Broxtowe Boy

Broxtowe Boy

by
Derrick Buttress

Shoestring Press

Typeset and Printed by Q3 Print Project Management Ltd, Loughborough (01509 213456)

Published by Shoestring Press
19 Devonshire Avenue, Beeston, Nottingham, NG9 1BS
Telephone: (0115) 925 1827
www.shoestringpress.co.uk

First published 2004
© Copyright: Derrick Buttress
ISBN: 1 899549 98 6

Shoestring Press gratefully acknowledges financial assistance from Arts Council England

To Joan, Kathryn, and Rachel

Acknowledgements

Short extracts from these memoirs were first published in *County Lit.* *The Interpreter's House*, and *The Coffee House* – to whom thanks are due.

Contents

Broxtowe Estate

We left the hidden back-to-backs,
the terraces and the rotten villages,
crossing the city
for a raw, enforced suburbia
and a settled life.

Carts and drays piled
with rough furniture and bundles
of bedding teemed
with kids and mongrels.
Here a man would be shaped
to his new home,
the women acquiescing
to new horizons.

But the men strolled leisurely
down to the pubs,
eyed abandoned tools
and planks lying around,
blind to the promise
of the future.

The roughest peed into the sink,
kicked their chickens
out of the kitchen
while their wives chopped out
the corporation fence for kindling.

And God, trying to love us all,
forgave us our first fights,
our foul mouths,
our total disregard
of his frail ontology.
For we go on being what we are,
always returning upon ourselves,
smashing the clock of good intent
we refuse to set our time by.

Chapter 1

Prologue

As a young man, Dad bore a slight resemblance to the Duke of Windsor and was considered by my Mam's sisters to be a smart dresser. He was particularly fastidious about his white shirts. He demanded a clean, starched collar every day, even though he was only a bus conductor working for the Corporation. Voices were raised, harsh words flew across the room if the collar of the day wasn't as white and stiff as he demanded. His final flourish before going out was to put on his soft trilby hat, adjusting it to an exact angle which I admired because it had the same rakish slant as George Raft's "nicky" hats in his gangster films.

Dad's concern for his appearance always irritated Mam. To her, it was a self-regard which diverted what she thought should be a proper concern for her welfare, as well as for my sister, Brenda and me. Yet, in spite of the rows it caused, I knew that Mam was pleased when her sisters commented on his style, and the fact that he looked like the Duke, even though she called him 'selfish'. Apart from income and status, there was one significant difference between Dad and the Duke of Windsor: the latter married for love; Dad married Mam because she was expecting me, and a quick wedding was the done thing when a boy got a single girl pregnant in 1931.

Mam was a good looking, fair-haired girl named Ada Radford from Hyson Green, an area of terraced houses and factories through which ran a broad street of shops, pubs and cinemas which buzzed with vibrant life, and was the center of the Radford family's world. It seemed logical to me as a child that the thoroughfare was named Radford Road. Mam was one of five sisters, loyal and supportive of

1

each other, and always ready for a sing-song when they got together in one of the Hyson Green pubs. There had been two Radford brothers: Arthur, the eldest child, served with the Northumberland Fusiliers and was killed at Soissons in 1918. His body was never found. I remember a dull bronze plaque the Government gave the family for their sacrifice of the 18 year old son and brother. The younger boy, Jack, died at the age of 17 from the lung-destroying gold leaf he worked with in the printing trade. Their father, Grandad Radford, survived the Great War as he had survived the Boer War, as a regular soldier in the Notts and Derby Regiment. But he succumbed, before I was born in 1932, to the wracking cough that was the aftermath of his being caught in a gas attack at the front. This annihilation of the men in the family created a protective bond between the sisters which was constant throughout their lives, an unquestioning friendship based on a mutual concern and the deepest of loyalties which their husbands were helpless against.

The Radford sisters didn't like Dad, much. They considered him too cold, too distant. But he was wary of all women, even when he was in the company of his own six sisters. They seemed "posh" compared to Mam's sisters, and they were more ambitious, more aware of making a good impression in front of neighbours and friends. They were working-class girls, but had set their sights higher under the tutelage of their mother, Grandma Buttress, whose father had owned once his own business as a cotton winder. In their eyes this made them a "cut-above" the Radford clan. My Buttress aunts were always kind to me, but their relationship with each other was often soured by petty jealousies. Dad rarely spoke about his sisters, or had much to do with them. It was almost as though he belonged to a different family, so lacking in ambition or personality was he compared to the popular Buttress girls with their sharp tongues and their good looks. One of them, also named Ada, won a national beauty contest in the early 1930's, but the others were just as attractive.

In 1931, Mam left her sisters and mother in the rough warmth of their cottage in Hyson Green to wait for my arrival in the attic of the Buttress terraced house. They had escaped the slums of Hyson Green to live in the slightly more substantial, more "respectable" streets of

New Basford in 1914. The class distinctions at the bottom of the social ladder were just as acute as those between the top and the bottom. The Buttress family went in fear of being considered "common". Their working-class origins must be disguised by a façade of neatness in appearance, but above all by their language and speech. The Radfords spoke in the flat vowelled, hard Nottingham dialect, a system of communication which ignored half of the syllabic content, running words together with an Anglo-Saxon efficiency in compounding sense. An inquiry such as: "Do you have any money on you?" would be rendered as "Ayyogorrowtonyer?"

Dad's sisters, cool in affection, but hot of temper, disdained the local dialect as the sign of "commonness". After all, their mother told them stories of her father, Samuel Morley, being a man of business, the friend of town councillors, a man who had been known to regularly hire a horse-drawn cab. These tales of a richer past took on the aura of a family myth. Perhaps it was the antidote to the fact that their own father, my Grandad, was a journeyman painter and decorator, an ordinary skilled artisan. But another family story was that he had once been in show-business as a child clog-dancer with a famous troupe called "The Ten Lancashire Lads", touring the music halls in variety. He claimed that he worked with Charlie Chaplin, also a member of the "Ten Lancashire Lads", and was taught a few steps by the great Fred Karno. His own father had acquired a fairground show called "The Anderson Circus" in the 1890's, the whole family performing in it as dancers and conjurers. I can still remember Grandad Buttress baffling me with disappearing coin tricks to liven up dull Sunday afternoons when I was very young. I like to think that those simple tricks linked me to the family circus. Even his name was baffling. Eventually I managed to sort out fact from myth: He was registered at birth as Harry Buttress; at his marriage he was Harry Maynard Buttress, the "Maynard" being his mother's maiden name. He added the name of the fairground circus, "Anderson" to his own name and dropped the "Maynard". For the rest of his life he was Harry Anderson Buttress, and he registered all of his ten children, including Dad, with "Anderson" as their middle name. This fact, I believe, was related to his assiduous reading of the "unclaimed money" column that used to appear in the *News Of The World* every Sunday, along with the family tale of Grandad's sister (yet another "Ada") running off to New Zealand with the profits of the "Anderson Circus". Grandad Buttress gave little away about his family, and the puzzle of the enforced name, along with the story of a missing inheritance is unsolved to this day, and is never likely to be solved, now.

The task of delivering me, late into a January night in 1932, fell to a tipsy midwife whose bungling almost finished me before I drew my first breath. Faced with the problem of a breach birth she tried to unscrew me into the world by grabbing my right foot and twisting it completely round. Grandma Buttress, alarmed by the prospect of losing her new daughter-in-law and a grandchild to this whisky-breathing incompetent, sent for a doctor who rescued both mother and child. I was placed in a blanket-lined drawer as a doubtful starter while he attended my mother.

In 1938 Mam and Dad separated for a year after their rows, usually about Dad's meanness with his meagre wages, and Mam's casual attitude towards falling into debt. Ironically, her attitude to debt would have been perfectly acceptable in this age of credit cards. But in the 1930's, owing 4 weeks rent, or several payments on the new three-piece suite was a frightening prospect for most people. I don't think it frightened Mam, but it certainly dramatized her marriage to a mean man. The climax to the drama came when Mam returned home to our house in Radford, after taking me to the cinema, to find a bailiff and several furniture removal men waiting for her in the parlour. She hadn't paid the hire-purchase for weeks, and they'd come to take the furniture away. If they hadn't been there, Dad would have probably murdered her. They separated, perhaps because they lost the house as well.

I went to live with Dad at his parent's house on Hollis Street in New Basford, where I was born. My sister, Brenda, went with Mam to live with her sister in Radford. I slept in the attic with Dad, was fussed over by Grandad and Grandma Buttress, and had two lively child aunts to look after me and take me with them on their outings. Aunts Dorothy and Violet recited the story of my hazardous birth with relish, conveying their sense of wonder at being twisted out of the womb, upside down. After that dangerous entry into the world, they were always benevolent towards me, displaying a kindness which they denied each other, for they were great squabblers. Dorothy was 14 years old, Violet was 12. I was treated as a younger brother, one who relied on them for affection, and was never disappointed. Their true brother, my father, they regarded then, and later, as an uncommunicative, stolid, uninteresting working man who had got himself into a mess because he wasn't as bright as them. They were always respectful towards Mam, as Grandad and Grandma Buttress were. But their very politeness indicated the distance which lay between Mam and themselves. My mother was an outsider, and would always remain one. After a year of separation, my parents were allocated a council house on the new Broxtowe Estate, built to accommodate families uprooted by slum clearance in the older areas of Nottingham, such as Sneinton and Radford. They key to a new front door meant they were giving their marriage a second chance. It also meant the happiest period in my childhood had come to an end.

Chapter 2

Broxtowe Estate

I clattered up the bare staircase, Brenda following slowly and with more decorum. The pungency of new wood mingled with the smells of fresh paint, here, as in the rooms downstairs. The new house was ours. No-one but the builders had ever set foot in it before. Mam was kneeling by the mysterious, dangerous-looking fireplace in the living-room, with a bundle of kindling, a screwed up copy of the *Evening Post* and some nuggets of coal she had carried from her sister's house on Hyson Green.

The first bedroom I entered seemed enormous compared to the attic I had been sharing with Dad in his parents' house on Hollis Street, two bus rides away. A small gas-fire was set into the wall – an amazing luxury for a bedroom.

"Come and look at this!" Brenda shouted from another room. I ran to her.

This room was smaller, even than the attic I knew so well. Fixed to the wall by the window was a handbasin with two shining chrome taps. Brenda was wrestling with the cold tap, trying to turn it on, but lacking the strength. "A sink in a bedroom!" she said, awestruck.

I knocked her hand away and turned the tap on. We watched the water swirl around the small basin, then gurgle noisily away. After the one-tap houses we had lived in before, such a facility in a bedroom seemed a reckless extravagance. I turned the tap off and we scampered, excited, into the third bedroom. This overlooked the small back garden which was divided from the garden opposite by creosoted palings. The room itself was square and characterless. We were disappointed to find no sink or gas-fire there.

We ran back to the bedroom with the gas-fire, obviously the main one. "This one's Mam and Dad's", Brenda declared, already bossy at six years of age.

"Alright, but I bags the one with the taps in," I said. We scuttled back down the stairs to report our discoveries to Mam.

The coals in the firegrate were smoking, but there was no flame to indicate the fire had taken. Mam knelt on the bare floorboards, her face set in concentration as she pushed a lever attached to the black canopy above the grate. It wouldn't do to interrupt her when she was so deep in concentration, and this strange looking fireplace was even more interesting than the bedrooms. There was a sudden rush of air in the grate that sucked smoke through a small arch set in the back. The roar made me jump back in fright. I thought the whole complicated contraption of doors and levers, made of shiny black metal, was going to explode. "What's it doing?" I shouted. "Switch it off, Mam! It'll blow up!"

"It's only drawing the fire," Mam laughed. And the coals ignited into welcome flame.

Seeing our own fire in the grate seemed to signify possession. This strange, luxurious house with its own concoction of new smells now belonged to us. The four of us living together again would be like the time we spent in the rambling house on Portland Road close to the city, which had come down in the world from the time when it was a middle-class residence, a house of empty rooms because Mam and Dad were too poor to furnish all of them. This new house on the Broxtowe Estate was a second chance, a new beginning. In the early Spring of 1939, I was seven years old, my pragmatic, sensible sister a year younger. We joined the exodus of families, most of them from the old slum areas, to the new estates west of the city. Nottingham had an admirable record of slum clearance and re-housing from 1919 until well into the 20th century. Broxtowe Estate was an expression of that pioneering energy in housing. It was built in ugly red brick, but designed with good intent, plotted and planned for a new way of life. Elliptical in pattern, its layout bewildered the stranger. Walk one of its streets without turning a corner, and you would always return to the spot you started from. The whole plan radiated from a featureless circle of grass called Denton Green. From it ran straight service roads bisecting those endless, uniform streets that would send you mad if you didn't know the escape routes.

The houses we had lived in before had only a stretch of pavement outside the front door, and a paved yard at the back. Now we had a square of rough, sandy earth at the front and rear which might be tamed enough to become a garden, some day. Brenda and I went outside to explore, scratching in a poor soil littered with builder's rubbish using pieces of wood left behind by the carpenters. We exposed broken bricks, bits of pantiles and slivers of glass. This, we thought, was gardening. Laboriously, we heaped the rubbish we had collected into a corner by the dustbin as evidence of our raw horticulture.

"Don't get yourselves dirty," Mam warned.

"We're doing the garden for Dad," I explained.

"Keep out of the way when the furniture van arrives," Mam said, then went back into the house.

Abandoning our gardening, Brenda and I ran to the front of the house to await the arrival of the van – a much more interesting task than dusty gardening. We couldn't have timed it better: the pantechnicon drew up at the kerb just as we reached the front gate. Dad was the first to climb out of the cab. "Don't get yourselves dirty," he said, which was more or less what we expected him to say. "Keep out of the way. And don't wander off."

I had grown used to Dad saying things like that. I don't ever remember him saying, "Would you like to do this? Would you like to do that?" No – it was always "Don't do this. Don't do that." It was automatic with him. Being a Dad, he seemed to think, meant telling your offspring not to do things.

We watched as the white-aproned removal men lugged our furniture into the house: a dining table and four chairs, two armchairs, a sideboard and three beds. We resumed our rubbish collecting to the sound of clanging bedsteads being assembled and shoved across the bare floorboards in the bedrooms.

We soon grew tired of harvesting the builders' junk. It was tedious work. "Let's make a path for Mam," Brenda suggested. We decided that one from the back door to the line post at the top of the garden would be most useful. After ten minutes of trying to arrange pantiles and broken brick into a path of some sort, the enormity of the task, as well as the tedium, made us abandon the idea. The strangeness of this new environment, the rawness and red-brick, suddenly brought on an aching homesickness for Hollis Street, especially for the company of my young aunts, Dorothy and Violet, who had known how to make life interesting. Dad's two youngest sisters were popular girls in their neighbourhood. Pretty, vivacious and energetic, they were fully involved in the youthful street life of Hollis Street and its neighbours. When I had lived there with Dad, they always took me with them into the street to join in the laughter, and the devilment. I had become spoiled by the attention their friends paid me, especially the boys, because making Dorothy and Violet happy seemed to be their main aim in life. Now, all that was gone. All I had was a pile of builder's rubbish, Brenda, and the oppressively quiet estate that offered no consolation.

But the unfriendly silence was suddenly broken. We heard a high pitched chorus of shouts, distant, yet plainly aggressive. It took a moment or two to locate the direction, so echoey were they. "Hark at them kids," Brenda said, just as startled as I was. We listened to the swell of young voices from somewhere beyond the furthest roofs we could see. There was anger in the shouting as if some mass argument was taking place. "Let's go and see!" I said, immediately forgetting Dad's instruction not to wander.

Dragging Brenda by the hand I tore across the open gardens in the direction I thought the yelling was coming from, seeking its source. We came out onto Bradfield Road, a thoroughfare which ran from Denton Green to the row of new shops at the other end. The raised voices were closer, now, and seemed to come from a building site beyond the last of the houses built. We ran across Bradfield Road and into the rough open space beyond. It was an overgrown meadow into which trenches had already been dug for new homes, the plan of each house clearly visible in the network of excavations and banks of soil thrown up by the digging.

Climbing the loose, sandy ramparts of a trench I surveyed the ground ahead, a little nervously. The shouting was louder now, and sounded more threatening. Beyond the builder's excavations lay a copse of weak looking birches. To the left there was a strip of woodland which looked dark and overgrown. On the right there was a curving road of new houses build of a lighter brick than ours, and looking somehow cheaper with what looked like metal window-frames. In the long grass ahead I could see figures moving cautiously forward. There was about a dozen of them, a battle line of boys throwing stones at adversaries I couldn't see, but guessed they were on the other side of the weedy birches. I watched the stones arc against a clear sky, then drop among or beyond the trees. Some retaliatory stones dropped and bounced between the stone throwers in front of me. One or two of the latter had slings, the crack of them scaring me. But I was too fascinated to duck back into my trench.

A cry of shock from one of the advancing gang startled me. He was a scruffy-looking boy a year or two older than me, I guessed. As he turned to run away from the line closing in on the trees I saw blood weeping from a gash on his forehead. Passing me, he glanced up. "The bastards hit me," he said without a tremor in his voice. I was deeply impressed by his stoicism, remembering the time when a toddler on Portland Road hit me over the head with a steel-bladed seaside spade, cutting me badly and sending me running home screaming blue murder. As I watched the wounded stone-thrower stumble over the building site I heard another cry. A thick-set boy in a ragged jersey was running from the battle clutching his head, although I could see no blood.

Brenda was still trying to clamber up the rampart, almost reaching the top before sliding back down into the trench. "Help me!" she pleaded querulously. "I want to see!"

"It's just a raid," I explained, wishing I hadn't burdened myself with a sister. "There's thousands of kids throwing stones at each other. Get some bricks for me to throw!"

I searched hurriedly in the sandy soil myself, exposing pebbles and larger stones by the dozen. I filled my trouser pockets then dropped a few inside my shirt. Brenda picked up the hem of her dress and dropped stones into the fold. When we had as many as we could carry we climbed over the ramparts then crept through the chest-high grass towards the front line. There was a lot of shouting, most of it in swear words I wouldn't have dared to use myself. Some of the shouting was part of a war of insults between the two gangs. Other shouts were yells of pain, or shock, as a missile struck somebody.

"That lad's bleeding," Brenda observed as another victim ran away clutching his head. I was comforted to see that this one was crying.

"Stay behind me," I ordered gallantly as we drew nearer the falling stones.

I was more scared of the rough faces and scruffy appearance of the boys than by the stones flying towards us and pitching into the deep grass close to us. One of the bigger boys saw us approach, noticed what Brenda was carrying in her dress. "Ammunition!" he shouted, and several of the scruffs ran up to us as we tipped out our stones at their feet. The raiders were flushed from their exertions, gathering our ammunition speedily, and without a glance at me before running back towards the trees, flinging the stones at an enemy I hadn't seen, yet. The big boy was obviously the leader. He was what Mam would have called "leary", a self-confidence which bordered on the arrogant. It was a characteristic I much admired, and dreamed of achieving myself, one day. He didn't look too concerned about the flying stones. He had a coolness about him which Buck Jones and Hopalong Cassidy would have been proud of. I could imagine that no danger would ever worry him. I wanted to join his gang right there and then. "Who are you throwing at?" I asked, timidly.

"It's them bastards from Westleigh Road. They're over in them trees. We've got 'em trapped. We're off Whitwell Road. You aren't off Westleigh Road, are you?"

I shook my head. "Never heard of it. We've just come to live on Frinton Road." I picked up one of the stones and lobbed it towards the trees. I was shamed to see it fly low through the air before dipping harmlessly into the grass before it reached half-way. The big boy laughed, then glanced down at Brenda. She was totally unconcerned about our danger, searching in the grass for stones.

"Is that your sister?" the boy asked.

"Yes. I've got to look after her." I thought for a moment he would turn me back because I had a girl in tow. "Can I be on your side?" I asked. "We can fetch you some more stones."

"Okay. But don't come any closer. And keep her out of the way – them stones hurt like fuck when they hit you."

He trotted off towards his advancing gang, yelling orders for a charge on the trees. I had never seen anybody as brave as him, except on the screen of the Bughouse, or the Electric Kinema, I grabbed Brenda's hand and ran after him. For the first time, I could see the enemy. The battle was virtually over. Beyond the copse lay a deep depression which might have been a quarry a long time ago. At the bottom, it was dark and spooky, overgrown with stunted bushes. One of the Westleigh Road gang was waving his shirt, but I didn't know if it was a signal of surrender, or defiance.

"If you want a truce, you can have one," our boy leader yelled down through cupped hands. "But we've won, though!"

"Bollocks!" one of the enemy shouted back.

"Give in, or we'll let you have it!"

There was a pause. The Westleigh Road gang seemed to argue among themselves, for a moment, then the one who had sworn answered. "Okay. We're coming out!" He still managed to sound defiant in spite of his helpless situation. "But don't throw at us when we come up. We're out of ammo."

"Okay." the big boy shouted. "Just keep off Whitwell Road in future!"

"You can fucking keep Whitwell Road," the beaten leader shouted.

The defeated gang struggled up a steep bank, slipping and sliding as they clung to weeds for support. There was about a dozen boys, most of them even scruffier looking than our lot. One of the smaller boys was crying, dabbing a dirty bit of rag to the back of his head as though he'd been hit. I suddenly felt sorry for them as they made their way towards the houses at the edge of the wasteland. One or two of our gang shouted in derision after them. Although I had felt a tinge of pity, I couldn't repress my elation that, in some small way, I also had been instrumental in defeating such a rough looking gang of boys, most of whom were older than me. It was a great first day in this new place.

There had been nothing like it in the innocent games played on Hollis Street, or the more refined Portland Road.

"We've won," I informed Brenda. But she wasn't interested. She had found a length of rope dangling from a low branch and was hanging on to it, the toes of her patent leather shoes just scraping the ground. As it passed me I grabbed it, joining her in the rope's slow rotations. The jubilant Whitwell Road gang rapidly dispersed towards the nearest row of houses, which I guessed was their road. The big boy was still leading them as they hooped and hollered their way home.

The rope stopped swaying. Brenda lightly jumped down. "I want to go home," she said. "Later. Let's play a bit. It's good here."

"I want to go *now*. I'm going to tell Mam you've been throwing stones," she said. "You'll cop it." She was growing increasingly aware that telling tales was a kind of power she could use to cut me down to size. So home we went.

She did report my stone throwing, but Mam was too tired to give me the slap I was expecting. Dad was more critical, though. "Keep away from the rough kids. They're all from Sneinton up the top end. They're too rough."

Sneinton was a notorious suburb close to the city – rougher even than Hyson Green. It bred hawkers, housebreakers and general miscreants with foul mouths and violent habits.

"You might've got your heads split open," Dad snapped. "You ought to have more sense."

It was an admonishment that he used with increasing frequency as I got older. But I didn't care. The battle had been fun. Broxtowe Estate was far from the scene of recent happiness, but it might be more interesting if my first day was anything to go by.

Chapter 3

1939

Mam was restless for a long time. Broxtowe was remote, an island of isolation far from Hyson Green. She missed the bustle of people with familiar faces who crowded the shops of her home ground: the general store called "Staddons" in which you could buy everything from a chamber-pot to a new rig-out for Saturday night; the fishmongers and the butchers shops with their small clouds of flies always in attendance. Most of all she missed the pubs where you could have a sing-song and see a fight at the same time. Broxtowe Estate she looked upon as her bad luck place, and she felt for years afterwards that Fate had placed her under a malevolent star when it forced her to live there. Like her sisters, she believed strongly in omens and signs. And her dreams told her that she was in for a hard time. Almost wilfully she fell behind with the rent. She deeply resented having to pay to live in a place that was unfriendly, and against her. It was only when her oldest sister, Liz, and her youngest, Mabel, joined Mam and another sister, Edie, on the estate that the pain of isolation was relieved, although her inability to pay the rent continued for many years. But that was due to her poor management of money rather than as an act of rebellion.

My new life began on the day we moved in. Quite soon, life on Hyson Green and Radford had become history as the slow-moving days and weeks drifted by. I went on long solitary walks to explore the area in spite of being told not to leave the safety of our own street. I fixed the boundaries of the territory I considered "safe" firmly in my mind. I would walk towards the dangerous "top end" as far as Denton Green. Our sister estate, Bilborough, was safe as far as my

Aunt Edie's house opposite the recently built John Player Junior School. To go beyond those two points was always a risk because the kids on any street at the "top end" were aggressively territorial, and might decide you were trespassing.

Bilborough was built of the same raw, reddish brick as the houses in Broxtowe, and the tenants were from the same old suburbs. Between the two estates ran an ancient country lane which connected Strelley Village to the roads leading into Nottingham. Strelley was still intact as a rural community, and made an attractive destination for those who wanted to get away from the monotony of the estates. Strelley was really a hamlet. Beyond its cluster of cottages, farm houses, pub and tiny schoolhouse lay Strelley Hall, a grey Georgian mansion guarded by high walls and locked gates. Inside lived Miss Edge, an elderly spinster with time on her hands, and many acres of parkland to spend it in. She once spoke to me, years later, and was kindly, pleasant and straight out of Jane Austen. She asked me what I did for a living. When I told her that I worked in a factory, she related that she, too, had visited one, once. The village church, All Saints, lay virtually in the grounds of Strelley Hall. Its weathered sandstone was pale gold in colour, and looked ancient. Inside its cold, rather creepy chancel lay an alabaster effigy of a medieval knight, one of the Strelley family. Beyond these two buildings lay parkland, plantations, woods and farms which made it, for me, the most beautiful spot on earth. Hyson Green, Radford and New Basford seems squalid in comparison. It became the place I loved most, after the Forum Cinema, and provided an escape from the rows at home, a place to explore, to birdnest, and to scrump. There was even a blacksmith in Bilborough Village, which I had to pass through to get to Strelley. He was a squat, surly malcontent who shouted at the estate kids to "clear off!" if we poked our heads round the open door of his forge to watch, awestruck, as he hammered red-hot shoes for the giant shire horses of Appleyard's farm. The days passed slowly in that first Summer, and outside of the house the world had become a fascinating place.

*   *   *

By the Autumn of 1939 my brother, Peter, had been born and Grandad's prediction that the politicians wouldn't be daft enough to allow another war to start had been proved wrong. The arrival of Peter was the bigger surprise to me. I hadn't known about it until Mam packed a bag to go into hospital for a few days. "You'll have a baby brother or sister when she comes home," Dad informed me, embarrassed at having to communicate such an intimate piece of news. I was in complete ignorance about the processes of pregnancy. Mam had just grown fat, as far as I was concerned, and Peter was an addition to the family she had decided on that week.

The black haired, red faced baby was fitted into the routine of our lives in August, then we concentrated on the possibility of us going to war against Adolf Hitler. Mam was worried, no doubt remembering her dead father and brother in the "first lot" as she called the Great War. Dad was as phlegmatic about the threat as he was about everything else.

"D'you reckon there'll be a war?" Mam asked him almost every day.

"Probably," he would reply without too much interest.

"D'you suppose you'll get called up, Hal?"

"I don't know," Dad would grunt from behind the *Daily Herald*.

I couldn't understand why he was so indifferent to the exciting prospect of war. As children, we absorbed the teaching that the British Empire was created as a result of the natural authority, the superior intelligence, and the military invincibility of the English race. After all, foreigners were nonentities who spoke in a barbarous gabble and waved their arms about, excitable and irrational. We English talked calmly and sensibly in a civilized language. I looked forward to the possibility of battle, thinking Adolf Hitler must be cranky to believe he could defeat our soldiers. It might take a little time because the Nazis looked pretty smart when they goose-stepped across the newsreels at the Forum Cinema, and they had given us a rough time in the "first lot". But a real war would be even more exciting than the Saturday afternoon serials. And it was inevitable that we would win simply because it was inconceivable that we could lose.

When Chamberlain made his funereal declaration of war we missed it because we didn't have a radio. Our neighbour, Mrs Marshall, shouted Mam out to relay the news in a frightened voice. Dad gave a disapproving "tut" when Mam relayed the news to him, and went into the kitchen to clean his shoes preparatory to going to the Beacon for his game of darts.

"How long d'you think it'll last, Hal?" Mam asked anxiously. "Will it be over by christmas?"

"I dunno," he said flatly. "Have I got a clean collar?"

When he had gone, Mam stood at the front room window staring out as if at some point beyond the clustered roofs. I was sure she was thinking about her brother, Arthur, whose death plaque lay wrapped in old newspaper on a shelf upstairs.

"When will they start shooting, Mam?" I asked.

"I bet they've started over there already," she answered. "I wonder how many poor devils are going to get killed in this lot?"

I went out to look for signs of the war, leaving her in a silence so deep I couldn't fathom it.

* * *

Adolf Hitler couldn't prevent the schools from opening up again after the Summer holidays. Although I was nervous about the prospect of a new school, I was also looking forward to it. I had changed school several times, and meeting new kids was always an act of discovery I enjoyed. My previous school, St Augustine's, was a five minute walk from Hollis Street, where I'd gone to live with Dad after his separation from Mam. It was a Victorian building of smoke-blackened bricks, with high windows. Its main classroom seemed to be perpetually dark. But I was happy there with a young female teacher whom I silently worshipped. We sat behind regimented rows of desks, learned the language of discipline, sat with folded arms to keep our hands from mischief when Miss was talking. On the wall facing us was a large, glossy map which Miss rolled down sometimes like a brightly patterned blind. Half of it seemed to be coloured red, and Miss informed us that the bright patches were the British Empire, exotic lands of vast wheatfields, endless prairies, and colourful natives who carried spears, and pounded their own corn. I felt enormous pride that I was part owner of such riches. On Empire Day we all stood to attention beside our desks and lustily sang *God Save The King*.

At Christmas, 1938, the teacher gave a party in the classroom. Wearing crepe paper hats, we ate a rich trifle concocted by the headmistress, who looked like a man with her short back-and-sides haircut and her faint moustache. Before the bell went to signal "hometime", Miss told us to sit quietly and listen. She switched off the lights. Miraculously, it had begun to snow. Huge feather-like flakes beat softly against the high windows, then slid down the glass. Then came the sound of reindeer bells, somewhere in the distance, and we held our breaths. A laugh boomed out, as a baggy-pants Santa Claus strode into the room with a huge sack on his back. Even my newly acquired scepticism about his existence couldn't spoil the moment. The excitement helped me to suspend my disbelief. As we slid across the melting snow of the playground on our way home we searched for reindeer hoofprints. I knew that we would never find them, but the search prolonged the party a few minutes longer. I knew, also, that the boy I walked home with was telling the truth when he reported that our Santa Claus had been the caretaker with a stuck-on beard. But the spell of that last innocent Christmas survived even his deflating realism.

At least there would be no more brief, and painful, reunions with Mam at my new school. During the time I lived with Dad on Hollis Street, Mam would walk from her sister's house on Hyson Green to wait for me at the school gate, usually at "hometime", but sometimes during "playtime". I would run to greet her when I saw her peering through the gateway. But my brief happiness at seeing her usually dissolved into tears when she turned to go after I had answered her questions about my well-being.

"I want to go with you, Mam!" I pleaded as I clutched her sleeve.

"I'll see you tomorrow," she always promised. "It won't be long."

"Come and live with us. Grandad'll let you!"

She would laugh at my naivity. But what she was feeling as she left me at the gate I will never know. It was history, now, and I had the prospect of a new school before me.

Player School, named after the family who owned the aromatic tobacco factory in Radford, was so new that part of it wasn't even finished. It occupied a site in Bilborough, the campus composed of two infant schools, two junior schools, one for boys and one for girls, as well as separate schools for senior boys and girls. I was to go into the class for the oldest children in the infant school, although I was old enough for the juniors. Brenda was placed in one of the normal infant classes. My classroom was filled with light from a row of french windows which opened onto what seemed an enormous space lying between us and the senior schools. It was the first time I had actually been able to look out of a classroom window. On the first morning I was too overcome by the natural brightness of the room to pay much attention to my new teacher. I spent most of the time watching a lumbering earth-moving machine chugging noisily in the muddy expanse beyond the infant school. Later, I learned that this huge machine with caterpillar tracks was digging air-raid shelters for us.

The lessons, also, were different. We were free to move from one group to another, the desks pushed together to allow our movement. The teacher never told us to sit with folded arms, or used the name of the headmistress as a threat. At St Augustine's we had to use their pencils, and return them at the end of the lesson. I once accidentally broke a pencil in half, and was caned for it by the teacher I worshipped. Here we were given a box in which we kept crayons, coloured pencils, plasticine and other educational delights. The only items we had to return at the end of a lesson were the scissors we used to cut up reams of coloured paper and board to make glue-sticky collages. The teacher, who seemed ancient to me, managed us with a gentle kind of firmness which nurtured my confidence. Several times a week we marched into the asphalt playground to do physical exercises with a plump, youthful teacher wearing shorts – a sight which made me giggle encouraged by a new friend, Alan, who also found it comic. She awoke in me more than laughter, though: I also felt a disturbing sensation which alarmed me by its pleasurable evil, and which embarrassed me enough to keep it from Alan.

Best of all I liked reading the illustrated story books which increased in difficulty according to the colour of the cover, but which I found easy to read even when I reached the hardest level, thus earning the privilege of being allowed to read any book I fancied. On Friday afternoons we packed away the scissors and glue, tidied our desks after a week's work as a prelude to listening to Miss read another episode of *Wind In The Willows*. This was the event I looked forward to all the week. The story totally absorbed me: Toad, Rat and Mole were as real as the kids around me as we listened, entranced, to the comic adventures of the three very English animals. There was a kind of magic invoked, the rhythms of the narrative were an incantation, hypnotic, summoning a response to the sound as much as the sense. The pleasure I felt awoke a need for language in me that must have lain dormant until the moment our skilful teacher read the opening sentence. When she closed the book for the week it was as if she had slammed the door on another, more pleasurable world, the images of which illuminated my imagination until the next reading.

When she finished the final sentence of the final chapter she smiled, as though in relief, and asked if we had liked it. I put my hand up and asked if she would read it again. She laughed, no doubt feeling that my request had answered her question, and promised that she would begin a new story the following week. She probably did, but I have no recollection of it.

Chapter 4

Looking for the War

So far the war had been a disappointment. Nothing had happened in
Broxtowe that was remotely dangerous. There had been no air-raids,
no church bells ringing out as a signal that the invasion of Britain had
begun. Even our gasmasks in their metal or cardboard containers had
become a burden as we carried them to school each day. Only the
aeroplanes flying over Broxtowe disturbed the peace. But they were
always "ours", and boys on the estate quickly developed their
aeroplane recognition skills as we craned our necks to observe
Spitfires, Hurricanes, Wellingtons and Whitleys, sometimes in flights
of three. The deep roar of a Spitfire engine would always set me
running for the garden if I was indoors. The "Spitty" was my
favourite aeroplane, the one I fantasised about. I was a flying ace, an
aerobatic show-off with a deadly aim when I had a Messerschmitt in
my sights.

Occasionally, a squad of soldiers would march along the lane
between Strelley and Broxtowe with a gang of estate kids imitating
their marching action, swinging their arms and stamping their feet in
time with the soldiers. Brenda and I followed one such march the
whole two mile length of Aspley Lane, which took us to the edge of
Radford. One of the weary soldiers threw us an apple, perhaps as a
reward for our endurance, and was yelled at by the red-faced sergeant.
The day was hot, the tar on the lane sticky in the heat, the men
sweating in their ugly uniforms. Their obvious discomfort undermined
my childish belief that our army was heroic, unbeatable, even, because
they, and we, were of a superior race. These men were just *ordinary*.
They were the same men I saw walking or cycling to work in their

overalls, the men in their best suits, their only suits, lounging outside the Beacon pub, or the Cocked Hat on a Sunday morning, smoking their cigarettes and shouting "Whoa" and "Hey up there!" to each other as they waited for the doors to open. In contrast, the Germans I had seen in the newsreels at the Forum Cinema wore more glamorous uniforms. Our soldiers wore uniforms which looked as though they would itch you to death, especially on a hot day. The Germans also had tommy-guns like the ones Chicago gangsters used. Most impressive of all were the tight riding boots the Nazis wore, and the way they stamped their feet in a frightening, choreographed goose-step that was sinister in spite of our mocking laughter at it. The men Brenda and I skipped alongside in our effort to keep up seemed to shamble clumsily in clod-hopper boots which looked like those worn by the scruffs at the top end of Broxtowe, and which they obtained with the aid of chits from the school welfare department. Being so close to them made them seem more human, but they certainly undermined my image, borrowed from films and stories, of the invincible British hero.

One day, an even closer encounter with our soldiers occurred as I crossed an abandoned building site at the bottom of Bradfield Road. There was a short-cut to the shops which everyone used. Two soldiers jumped from the back of a truck and began to dig a slit trench across the short-cut path. I, and a gang of estate kids who seemed to *know* something unusual was happening, arrived before the soldiers spades had lifted the first matted sods of the path. We formed a circle around the soldiers, convinced that the invasion of Britain was about to start. Were we to be the witnesses of Nazi paratroopers fluttering down on Broxtowe estate in their fancy boots? Sweating in front of an audience of excited, scruffy kids must have got on the soldiers' nerves because they kept telling us to "bogger off". But there was no way we were going to miss out on the invasion. This was better than a front seat at the Forum.

When the soldiers were satisfied that the trench was deep enough, they leaned on their shovels and had a smoke. In a little while the truck was backed up to the trench and a bren-gun hauled out. The soldiers set it up at the edge of the trench. The crowd grew bigger; the soldiers more annoyed. Even women with shopping bags were affected by our curiosity and leaned over our heads to peer at the gun. This was a thrill – our first sight of a weapon!

"When are you gunna shoot it, mate?" a boy asked in happy anticipation.

"When I get some bullets."

"Who're you gunna shoot?"

"You'll be the first if you don't sod off," the soldier said, fed up.

We watched as he adjusted the sight of the bren, aiming it at the corner around which women trudged with their heavy shopping bags. A fussy woman from a house across the road brought over two mugs of tea which the soldiers drank leisurely as we fretted for the gun to be fired. It never was.

After what seemed like hours, the bren-gun was loaded back into the truck, and the soldiers left without a word or a glance at us. Most of the crowd dispersed, but I and a few more disappointed kids stared down into the rough trench. All we could see were the dog-ends of the soldiers' cigarettes, and sliced roots which must have nourished trees when Broxtowe was a rural place. The trench became just another hole in the "humps and hollows" of the forgotten building site. And the only action I saw that day was the swipe Mam gave me for taking so long to run a simple errand.

I searched for the war everywhere. But I could find it only in newspaper reports and on the newsreels at the Forum. My schoolmates and I had to do with imaginary wars fought out in the fields, woods and abandoned building sites which served as battlegrounds. So far, few of the men who were our neighbours had been called up. Mr Marshall, a toolmaker in a gas-meter factory, was in a reserved occupation and would never be called up. He even managed to play cricket, cycling off in his whites, knowing he would never have to change them for a khaki uniform. Joe Peach, whose house backed onto ours, had poor eyesight and wore spectacles of thick glass which magnified his eyes alarmingly. He cycled off to his night-shift at the Co-op bakery, close to Trent Bridge, as usual. Dad was still punching tickets on the corporation buses.

The prospect of danger looked more promising when the clatter of sheets of metal being thrown together disturbed a dull morning. I ran out of the house to find out what was going on, thinking, for a moment, that a bomb might have dropped. What I saw were shining, silvered corrogated steel sheets being stacked on the front garden. The Anderson air-raid shelter had arrived. I raced indoors to tell Dad, but he merely tut-tutted in his usual way. He always greeted the unusual with a dispiriting lack of interest. However, he couldn't dampen my enthusiasm for this welcome evidence that we, too, were part of this war. I even volunteered to help him carry the steel into the back garden, an offer which only seemed to irritate him more.

Dad had dug the back garden, but the soil was poor. A thin layer of top soil hid what was, basically, sandstone which he lifted on his spade in crumbling chunks. The thought of having to laboriously dig through three feet of it made him almost despair. "How'm I supposed to dig through flaming rock?" he complained after he had skimmed off the top soil.

Joe Peach was setting his shelter close to ours, only the picket fence separating his from Dad's. Joe was a short, cheerful man who was always ready for an over-the-fence chat with Mam, who found him comical. He whistled chirpily, swinging a pick at his unyielding patch of sandstone. Dad banged at his in a temper, his spade breaking up the shard-like fragments which he scooped up to toss onto the evergrowing heap beyond the rectangle he had marked out for the shelter. He rarely swore, choosing instead to express his frustration through deep sighs and shakes of his head.

After he had loosened his patch with his pick, Joe took a rest, leaning on the fence to watch Dad's struggles. "You won't get far like that," he said cheerfully. "You need a pick."

"I haven't got a pick," Dad grunted. He lit a cigarette, seating himself on the edge of the shallow pit for a rest. He certainly wouldn't ask if he could borrow Joe's pick. He never asked anyone for anything.

"You can borrow mine in a bit," Joe said, not put off by Dad's curt manner.

Dad was always embarrassed by such friendly overtures. He was bad at being sociable. He would have preferred to be left alone to labour in his own way. "Ta," he said with as much grace as he could muster.

Setting up the air-raid shelter took a few days, but finally it was completed and the sandstone thrown over it. We never used it, though. Mrs Marshall asked Mam to join her in theirs because her husband sometimes worked a night shift, and she would be afraid on her own. Mr Marshall had lavished a craftsman's care on his shelter: it was thoughtfully provided with blankets and pillows for the bunk beds. He had fixed an electric light from the supply in the house, laid straw matting on the floor and knocked up a wooden door in the entry vent (although this was dangerous as a nearby blast could have sent fatal splinters flying into the shelter). Our shelter slowly grew dank, and a pool of water formed. Then we used it to dispose of rubbish from the garden, I found it an ideal place in which to keep toads. They were always to be found in the hedge bottoms on rainy nights. I loved holding them, and kept one in my pocket as a pet until somebody told me that they exuded a white substance from their knobbly backs which gave you incurable warts. Finally, I was the only person who dared to go down into the shelter, even Dad wouldn't jump into it, habitated as it was by cockroaches and amphibians. When the shelter was taken down, and the pit filled in years later, relics of my childhood were buried under that impoverished soil, including the fragile bones of forgotten toads.

The first air-raid, when it finally came, trapped me in limbo. I thought it would burst on us dramatically at night accompanied by the crashing of the ack-ack battery recently installed in a field just beyond Bilborough Wood. We would hear the cries and whistles of steel helmeted wardens as they raced up and down the streets, urging us into our shelters. I had played the scene out many times in my head, because I was looking for a chance to be a hero. I would survive Adolf Hitler's bombs. I couldn't conceive of myself as a victim. I would be the begrimed rescuer tunnelling into a neighbour's flattened house because I was the only kid brave enough to crawl into holes too small for the wardens.

What actually happened was that I was caught out at a moment when Alan and I were splashing each other in a rain puddle as we made our way home from school at lunchtime. A shower had passed, allowing a watery sun to break through. Then the lugubrious moan of a siren wound up the air, climbing to an eerie wail then down again, repeatedly. For a few seconds we were transfixed by the shock of the sinister noise rolling over us. Alan was staring at me, paralysed. Brenda, who had been disdainfully watching our splashing game, began to whimper. A stout woman in a headscarf and carrying a loaded shopping bag broke into a flat-footed waddle down the road. "Gerrof home!" she shouted over her shoulder. "It's an air-raid. The Jerries are coming!"

The tone of adult panic in her voice triggered our own fear. As a group of senior girls ran past, screaming, Alan and I followed them, splashing through puddles and hurtling across Broxtowe Lane without looking. Brenda was crying because of the rough treatment she was getting as I dragged her, stumbling, behind me. I was excited, yet afraid, not daring to look up into the ever-widening lagoons of clear blue sky in case I would see the black silhouette of a German bomber.

Mam was waiting at our gate in a disappointingly calm manner as we raced down Frinton Road to the dying moan of the siren. "It's an air-raid, Mam!" I yelled as we approached her. "Get down the shelter, quick!"

She herded us up the path towards the back of the house. "Your feet are wet through," she complained. "What've you been playing at?" We climbed through the strung wire fence dividing our house from the Marshall's, raced across the garden, then dived into the shelter. "Take them shoes off. You ought to have more sense," Mam persisted. "It's a good job your Dad's not in."

Her reproach seemed grossly unfair. I might even now, I thought, be tunnelling through the debris of a wrecked house. And hadn't I saved Brenda? Here she was in her shiny black ankle-strap shoes and spotless white socks clinging to Mam's arm with a smug smile on her face because my shoes were being examined with sour disapproval. "They're ruined," she moaned. "I've a good mind to paste you!"

Mrs Marshall gave me a wink of support. She was always kind to the Buttress kids because she was childless herself.

"Was you frightened?" she asked.

"No," I lied. "Brenda was though. But I looked after her."

As Brenda didn't object to this claim, Mam must have believed me. It was either that or the welcome wail of the all-clear siren that saved me from the threatened pasting. I was sent back to school in a pair of plimsolls, resenting the anti-climax of a raid in which nothing happened. We weren't even allowed a proper air-raid, and it seemed like a piece of personal bad luck. Alan offered the only glimmer of hope as we trudged back to the Player School. "Jerry might come tonight," he said. "I bet the A.R.P. are expecting them. That's why they had a practice on the sirens."

"They won't bomb Broxtowe," I complained. "There's nothing worth bombing."

"What about the guns down Bilborough? I bet Jerry knows they're there by now. He'll be after them."

We lived in hope of action. So far the war had been a washout. It was like sitting in the Forum and finding that they'd lost the film.

Chapter 5

The Kews

The Radfords gathered as a clan again when Mam's eldest sister, Liz Kew, was moved out of her condemned house in Clayton Square, close to the city, and was allocated a council house in the rougher "top-end" of Broxtowe. Now there were three sisters within calling distance of each other: my Aunt Edie, Mam, and the formidable Liz. Dark haired, unlike her younger sisters, full bodied and awkward in movement, Liz had developed a deadly cutting edge in her voice as if to compensate for her slow-moving bulk. With this weapon she managed to exert her authority from a sitting position, occasionally accompanying her vocal threats with a body feint as if she was about to leap from her chair. She never did, being incapable of such sudden action. Neither her husband, George, nor her three children opposed her because she had her head screwed on right, and had more sense than the rest of them put together. She also made them laugh with her scathing observations of other people's vanities and idiosyncrasies, and they didn't want to be her next victim.

Dad said nothing when he heard the news of Mam's reinforcements arriving, but I had learned to read the smallest changes of expression in his face – the tightening of the mouth always signalled his disapproval. He probably felt threatened by his sisters-in-law. They were Mam's confidants, her support in her complaints about his meanness both with money, and in his behaviour towards her. He was wary of Aunt Liz in particular, and was diplomatic enough not to have rows with her. She, like her sisters, would not row with Dad for Mam's sake. It would only make matters worse because Dad would seek his revenge by threatening, or even hitting, Mam. Thus the relationship between Dad and his sisters-in-law limped on – polite, distant, yet in an atmosphere of mutual, unspoken dislike.

Like Mam, I was delighted that the Kew family had moved so close to us. In the past I had spent entertaining, carefree hours in their tiny house in Clayton Square, set in deepest Radford. The Square was no more than a courtyard of mid-nineteenth century back-to-back cottages in one of the poorest parts of Nottingham. It had been condemned in the 1920s, but it was 1940 before the families were moved out. It was still standing in the 1950s, and the houses occupied by young couples waiting for a council house in the desperate post-war years of a housing shortage. Like other small, decaying but self-sustaining areas of the city, Clayton Square and the surrounding streets had the ambience of an urban village. When the inhabitants of the Square declared that they were going "down town" they were speaking of a journey which took no more than fifteen minutes on foot, yet one which took them to a world of unattainable affluence far away from the one downstairs room with its tapless sink, its gaslight, and its crumbling plaster beneath the cheap wallpaper. When they returned, emerging from the darkness of the narrow entry into the Square, the first thing they saw was the single cold-water tap screwed to a post in the middle of the yard, next to the single gaslamp. This tap served all the houses and was the only source of water. The only other amenities were a brick washhouse and some communal lavatories.

Now that the Kews had exchanged that decaying world for the modern plumbing and spacious rooms of a Broxtowe "double" council house, I would see more of Ida, my cousin, a girl in her early teens, but a motherly, warm natured girl with a quick smile and an even temper. I loved being left in her capable hands when our parents strolled off on their Saturday night migration to the Beacon or the Cocked Hat. She taught me the words of heart-rending ballads such as We'll Meet Again and Don't Go Down To The Mine, Dad. She made their excruciating sentimentality sound so convincing that we finished up sobbing together, while Brenda looked on with a rationalist's disdain.

I never thought of Cousin Ida as a child, like me. She was too responsible, too wise – apart from her taste in music. Her sole concern when given the task of caring for Brenda and me was to amuse and

29

entertain us. When I was five years old she had plonked me on the bed in her attic room in Clayton Square to tell me a story, a true one. I listened, enthralled as she related the tale of a poor, young Welsh miner called Tommy Farr who had sailed across the Atlantic Ocean to challenge a mighty black fighter called Joe Louis for the heavyweight championship of the world. For her the match was a romance that had resonances which echoed in her own life: her father, too, was a miner, and her brother was a boxer whose name was Tommy. A boy who might have felt at home in Clayton Square had taken on the rich and the powerful in distant, mythical America. She told me the story on the day before the fight took place. We were convinced it would have the happy ending of all fairy stories. But when morning came Ida woke me up to report, tragically, that Tommy Farr had been cheated by the referee after having boxed Joe Louis's head off. She cried, and I cried with her because I hated to see her unhappy.

Tommy, Ida's brother, was a good-looking, blonde youth with so much confidence in himself that Mam thought him leary, though his cheekiness was amiable enough at that time. Aunt Liz doted on him. He was a "real lad", one who knew how to take care of himself in a hard-nosed world, and if his cockiness got him into trouble sometimes, well, it was what bubbly 16 year olds did because it was in their nature. He fought as an amateur for the Raleigh Boxing Club. When he won a fight he would return home with a trophy, a shiny, plated cup or an ornate biscuit barrel which he would give his mother because he had done it for her, and she would display them on her sideboard to show what a character her son was. Tommy's ambition was to join the Royal Navy because it was a man's life and he knew that with his defiant grin and lithe, athletic body he would look good in uniform. Tommy was, unknowingly, enjoying the most successful years of his life then. Some weakness in his character, perhaps an expectation that the rest of the world was going to treat him with the same doting indulgence as his mother, or a belief that he could charm himself out of trouble with a cavalier smile and cheeky repartee, proved to be his undoing because his life became harder, and more cruel, than he had imagined.

*   *   *

Uncle George, Ida's father, was a wiry little man whose dour expression and rough, laconic style of commenting on the world and of conversing with his family made me feel just a wee bit nervous of him. Although he could make you laugh with his dry humour, that dour expression signified that he wasn't the sort of man you upset without risk of a verbal lashing. Small in stature he might have been, but he was tough and had the miner's compacted strength. The house the family had been allocated backed onto Broxtowe Wood, a large plantation of mature pines Uncle George explored with a glint in his eye. Shortly afterwards he came home with a brand new lumberjack's axe, and I followed him about as he tried it out on one of the smaller pines.

When the sections of his Anderson air-raid shelter arrived he gazed down on them with contempt, an attitude he always emphasized by shooting a huge gob of phlegm. "They're no bleddy good," he swore. "You waint stop blast with tin cans!" I believed him because he had fought in the Great War as a boy soldier who, like so many, had lied about his age. What had really inspired this rejection of Mr Anderson's gift was, probably, a burning desire to use that lumberjack's axe in a constructive way. Thus he declared war on lovely Broxtowe Wood. I followed him as he pushed through the undergrowth, expertly measuring the tall pines with what looked like an expert eye. Then he began his attack. I had to watch from the safety of the boundary fence after he ordered me not to follow him or get in his way. A few nosy "top-end" boys wandered into the wood after him. But he gave them his stoniest look and they, too, retired to the sidelines. The speed and efficiency with which he felled his first towering tree made me wonder if he hadn't been a lumberjack at some time in his life. His small, well-set figure looked puny against the pine. He swung his axe against the thick trunk, sending wedges of white chippings flying through the air like shrapnel. When he had made his precisely calculated 'V' shape cut he went to work with a long, double-handed saw to complete the destruction. He never seemed to pause for rest. As the great tree slowly crashed through the branches of other trees in a tearing, splintering fall to earth he hardly moved, so accurate was his calculation.

At school I overheard one of the top-end boys tell his pals about the man in Broxtowe Woods who could chop down a tree in the time it took you to go to the lavatory and back. "I went home to have a quick one while the bloke was still chopping. But when I got back to the wood the tree was flat on the ground." I told him the axeman was my Uncle George because I detected the tone of admiration in the telling of the story and was able to enjoy a moment of reflected awe, as well as make a new pal.

After Uncle George had chopped down sufficient trees for his needs, he began to strip them of their branches with swift, accurate strokes of his axe until he had reduced the trunks to what looked like rough telegraph poles. He allowed me into the wood to help him clear the branches before he set to with his saw, cutting the trunk and some of the bigger branches into measured lengths. I had no sense of the destructiveness of his work, marred now by stumps and fallen branches entangled in the undergrowth. His desecration signalled the beginning of the end for the wood, its darkness now pierced by dramatic shafts of light from the newly exposed sky. Soon, anyone who owned a household hatchet joined in the assault on the trees so that they could stoke up the fires of winter with free, violently spitting pine logs.

The tedium of stripping the trees, and getting scratched to bits dragging the rough-hewn poles through the undergrowth, made me stay away for a day or two. I didn't go back until Mam sent me on an errand, her message scribbled on a scrap of paper was the usual one: *Dear Liz, can you lend me a £1 till Friday. You'll get it back, Ada.* Cousin Ida ran to meet me as I pushed open their front gate. "Come and look at our air-raid shelter!" she urged, dragging me round to the back of the house. At the bottom of their uncultivated patch of back garden was the top half of a perfect, flat-roofed log cabin set in a pit deep enough for an Anderson shelter. It filled the air with a wonderful scent of pine.

"What do you think?" Ida asked, obviously proud of her father's handiwork.

"Is it allowed?"

"I don't know." Ida laughed. "That won't bother me dad."

Aunt Liz shuffled out of the kitchen to join us. "I don't know how I'm supposed to get down that thing," she complained. The drop down to the entrance was considerable and would require a jump, or a long stretch of the legs. There were no steps. Suddenly, Uncle George poked his head out of the entrance – I hadn't realized that he was down there.

"You'll get down quick enough if Jerry drops a bomb on you!" he shouted down the garden.

"I bleddy waint!" Aunt Liz shouted back. "You waint get me down no air-raid shelters. Bogger Hitler and his bombs!"

Uncle George retreated back into his cabin, swearing to himself. "Looney bogger," Aunt Liz muttered scathingly as she waddled back into the kitchen to read Mam's note. Already I was dreaming of the games I could use the cabin for. How many kids had the use of a frontier post? It was the perfect place for last ditch stands against Apaches, Zulus and Nazis. What a pity Cousin Ida wasn't a boy. Unfortunately, Uncle George soon put paid to my schemes. He gave me strict orders not to go into the air-raid cabin and, wary of the withering look he gave me, I obeyed.

The pine-log cabin was a seven-day wonder, then it was ignored even by Uncle George who had become preoccupied with his rabbit poaching, his spare time spent mending the holes in his nets. The cabin slowly merged into the garden until it seemed to have returned to nature, a pile of peeling logs and poles half hidden in a mound of earth, and the garden's luscious weeds.

* * *

Aunt Liz's eldest child was named Arthur after her dead father and brother. In Mam's system of superstitious belief, which was ruled by Bad Luck and his sister Good Luck, naming an offspring after the deceased was a rash invitation to the dark star of Illness, son of Bad Luck, to exert its power. When Arthur, as a young boy, suffered a severe bout of pneumonia which left him with a weak heart, Mam felt that her faith in a primal, spiteful Fate had been justified. He was closer to his sister, Ida, in temperament rather than to Uncle George or Tommy. A gentle natured, good humoured and slow moving young man, he ignored the gap of a generation between us, treating me as an equal. Often out of work due to his illness, he discovered the escapist pleasures of pulp fiction, enjoying American thrillers, especially. He lost himself in stories which featured blondes in flimsy silk blouses which always got torn off at a climax by hard-bitten, monosyllabic private "dicks" who carried snub-nosed .38 revolvers. When I became proficient enough in my reading to join him in this study of the American underworld, Arthur passed on the dog-eared novelettes to me. Soon, I too was an expert of the genre. Our criteria for judging a novelette's quality was simple: if we had worked out who had done the murder before the last page, we considered the story a dud.

The conventions of spare, gutter prose was meat and drink to us. Our pleasure was immeasurably increased when the style and the convention was magically transformed into moving images on the screen of the recently built Forum Cinema, or on the smaller screens of the old cinemas on Hyson Green, the Boulevard (which everybody knew as the Bughouse), Lenos and the Grand. In Edwardian times, the Grand had been a theatre on whose stage a teenaged Charlie Chaplin had cavorted with his brother, Sid. Lenos, named after the famous comedian, was one of the oldest cinemas in Nottingham. These dark, seedy bolt-holes were cramped, egalitarian in their discomfort, but cheap to enter. There was always a reek of stale Woodbine and Park Drive smoke, the sickly perfume of flea exterminator, as well as the oily aroma of girls doused in *Evening In Paris* scent, which the local lads re-named *Evening In Grimsby*. The scent was bought in a sixpenny phial from the Hyson Green Woolworths. If we were bored by a love scene, or the film was British, which to us youthful critics was synonymous with rubbish on account of the actors' excruciating English accents, we could chat to our pals, borrow a cigarette or ask for a toffee from some pal we had spotted trying to chew a caramel without being seen. At moments of high passion on the screen somebody always farted or shouted obscene sex instructions to the virginal looking hero. That would provide a cackle of coarse laughter which would send the old doorman in his braid cap running up and down the aisles in his search for the culprit.

We were in the "golden age" of the cinema, although we didn't know it and thought it would go on for ever like this. The actors were mythical, as far from our narrow lives as it was possible to get. The world in which they moved, whether it was a sleazy nightclub full of gangsters or a vast, chandeliered hall which was the average American living-room, was as fantastic and insubstantial as our wildest dreams. Sometimes the films tortured us; why were their cliff-sized chunks of cake at cocktail parties so soft and creamy when we couldn't even find the currants in our dry slabs bought from the Co-op? And why didn't they ever eat it? There were times, deep into a supperless evening, when we would have sold our sisters for a slice of such rich confectionary. Even worse for the apprentice smokers was seeing the king-sized cigarettes so casually discarded after just one puff: light-puff-stub, light-puff-stub. On it went in film after film while the khaki fingered mob of nicotine addicts in the Forum or the Bughouse scorched their lips on a quarter inch of Woodbine picked from the detritus under the seats.

These womb-like fantasy palaces were Cousin Arthur's haven, his means of escape from the meanness of Hyson Green and the indifferent world that kept it, and him, in place. Hollywood and pulp fiction fed his imagination, but denied him the growth into the person he might have become. As a boy he had passed an exam to go to secondary school, but Aunt Liz couldn't afford to send him, although the Radfords, including Mam, thought education of little importance. He responded to the tawdry arts because there was no other world open to him. Reality was mean enough when he was young. But as ill-health closed off more of the world to him he made a private one for himself composed of cheap dreams.

Chapter 6

Call Up

The buff envelope delivered that morning was important looking, obviously something from above, official and demanding. Mam usually screwed such communications up and tossed them on the fire even when they were addressed to Dad, as this one was. Sometimes the envelopes contained a notice-to-quit from the council because the rent hadn't been paid. More often they were threats from the County Court to pay a long-standing debt owed to the tallyman for furniture or clothing. Mam was always in debt because Dad never gave her enough out of his wages to pay her way. Often she would take out a "cheque" which enabled her to purchase essentials on a live-now-pay-later basis. Her problem was that she never had enough money in her purse for the pay-later part of the deal.

She didn't destroy this letter because she seemed to know what it contained, and it wasn't connected with debt. She placed it on the table propped up against the sugar bowl and kept glancing at it nervously. When Dad came in and opened the letter he actually smiled, not with pleasure: his expression was too bleak for that, but as if to acknowledge the awesome persistence of the family's bad luck. "It's my call up," he muttered. "I've got to report next week." He laughed dryly, then bit into his toast.

"There's plenty who should go before you," Mam said. "What about these blokes without any kids? There's plenty of them walking about. What about all these skivers in reserved occupations? They ought to sort some of them out first," she complained bitterly.

"I don't know," Dad said. "I'm not the government. Ask them."

"It's not fair." Mam moaned. "How am I supposed to live on a soldier's pay?"

Dad was irritated by her insistence on discussing it. He wanted to read his *Daily Herald*.

"Others manage, so you'll have to."

It was Dad's usual fatalistic response to the demands of authority. As far as he was concerned you did what you were told because there was less fuss that way. His parents told him he would have to get married when he made Mam pregnant with me, and he did. Now that the government had told him that he would have to exchange his bus-conductor's uniform for a khaki one, well, it was useless to complain. There was no point in talking about it.

When he came back from registering, he told Mam that he had put his name down for the Royal Horse Artillery because the blokes waiting in the queue for the other regiments had looked a "pack of riff-raff". At the moment of his departure he kissed Mam with a tenderness that shocked me. I'd never seen that before. I went out into the garden, awkward and embarrassed by their show of affection. Mam was crying when I came back, and I was puzzled, and wondered if I knew as much about them as I thought. Perhaps for that moment they had recovered some feeling about each other they had once, but had lost.

Mam's youngest sister, Mabel, had seen her husband give up driving his lorry for the corporation parks department to drive one for the Sherwood Foresters a few weeks before Dad went. Plump, blonde and excitable, Aunt Mabel resented her husband being taken from her, and made more fuss than Mam. Uncle Herbert was tall and handsome with black wavy hair. He laughed in a cheerful baritone at Aunt Mabel's comic nagging. She worshipped him, and he in his turn was always affectionate, called her "Mib" and allowing himself to be ruled by her without the slightest dent in his masculinity or geniality. He joked her out of her bad moods and shared her good ones, making her laugh and paying her the kind of attention I had never seen Mam receive from Dad. Herbert was Mam's favourite in-law, the only one Dad really liked.

Within the sisterly bond of the Radford girls, the relationship between Mam and Aunt Mabel was so close it seemed to exclude their own children. Circumstances dictated by "bad luck", had forced

Mam to draw on an inner strength, a peasant fortitude inherited from her frameworker ancestors for whom poverty was endemic. That strength had enabled her to survive the hard knocks she had taken so far, and would have to take in the future. Aunt Mabel, being highly strung, was a passionate victim of panic and anxiety when the calm surface of her life was disturbed. It was at such moments that she sought refuge in Mam's strength. Her uncertainties were quelled by Mam's reassuring prediction that everything would come out right in the end, at least for her sister who was born under a luckier star than herself. Herbert would survive the war without harm (he even survived the Anzio beachhead). There wasn't a German bomb with "a present for Mabel" written on it. Then they would have a cup of tea before Aunt Mabel returned home to Radford, placated, smoothed over and glad to have someone as patient and comforting as her sister, Ada, to see her through the war.

* * *

Cousin Tommy, who had fretted impatiently for his seventeenth birthday to arrive, was old enough at last to join the Royal Navy. He became the third member of the family to leave for the war. By 1941 it seemed as if the conflict had become a tangible event, and not something distant, and remote. I followed the news in the local *Evening Post* and in the national *Daily Herald* and was convinced that we were winning, even though it was a close call. According to the newspapers and the cinema newsreels, the disaster of Dunkirk appeared to be a victory; Winston Churchill was confident; the air-raids on London only made the cockneys cheerful and chirpy. They were always photographed with their thumbs up, beside bombed-out shop windows which displayed the notice *Business as Usual* written on rough bits of wood and stuck in the debris. The occasional warning on the siren usually signalled a non-event, although the ack-ack battery in Bilborough blasting away at planes we couldn't see or hear made me wonder if that wasn't overdoing the excitement a bit. In the evenings I enjoyed watching the long, probing beams of searchlights as they crossed and recrossed the clear sky in ever-changing patterns of light.

One night the racket from the guns was so powerful and persistent, Mam, Brenda and I bolted in panic, bare footed, for Mr Marshall's shelter dressed only in our nightwear. We shivered in darkness because Mrs Marshall was too scared to have the light on. "They're just passing over," Mam said to calm her, which was generally the truth. The guns reached a powerful crescendo, a shocking blast followed seconds later by the crack of bursting ack-ack shells overhead. There was a lull in the guns' turmoil, and in that brief silence I heard the strange, unsynchronized moan of aircraft engines. So different was the sound, I knew immediately that the planes were German, Heinkels or Dorniers.

"Listen!" I urged. "German bombers!"

Mrs Marshall gave a little cry. "I can hear them!" she wailed. "They're right over us!"

"They're not Germans," Mam said, and seemed annoyed by my lack of tact. "They're our lads."

"They're not," I persisted. "The engines are going der-der-der-der. That's how Jerry planes go."

"Well if they are," Mam snapped, "They're just passing over, so shut up!"

The next morning I caught up with Alan on the way to school.

"Did you run to the shelter?" he asked as we hunted for shrapnel in the gutter.

"We couldn't get down quick enough. It was a bit scary. Did you hear the Jerry planes?"

"Yeah, great, wasn't it?"

We imitated the moan of German engines until Alan suddenly leapt across the pavement to pick up a fragment of shining, jagged metal gleaming under a privet hedge. He dropped it immediately with a cry of pain. "Blimey – it's still hot!"

Slivers of ack-ack shells which quickly turned from silver to rust. Bullet cases of brass that you stood on end for your schoolmates to aim marbles at. The searchlights' free show most nights, and silver barrage balloons swimming comically on the breeze. Bored soldiers staring bleakly out of the backs of passing trucks, or clomping down to the Beacon with their Dads, their mates or their wives when they were on leave. Letters from Dad, Uncle Herbert or Tommy *Sealed With A Loving Kiss*, and everywhere sandbags, in the doorways of street air-raid shelters, around fire-alarms and school stirrup pumps. The war was visible now, an intrusion into the landscape, a system which governed our lives. We settled into its routine of queues, rations and air-raid warnings, read the euphemistic exhortations of posters on how to survive. The system offered security against the threat of catastrophe inherent in the wail of the siren and the searchlights' neurotic sweep of the night sky.

> *SWITCH THAT LIGHT OFF!*
> *DON'T FORGET YOUR GAS MASK!*
> *CARELESS TALK COSTS LIVES!*
> *PARSNIPS CAN TASTE LIKE PINEAPPLE –*
> *GET THE LEAFLET!*

We knew we were being looked after. As long as we read the ubiquitous posters we would win through. Churchill was a hero, and heroes always won in the end. Hadn't the pictures on the Forum taught us that? When we sang along with the dancing dot over the cheery words on the screen between films, we knew Adolf Hitler was done for.

The air-raid warnings continued throughout the spring, although few bombs had been dropped on Nottingham so far. The armageddon which had devastated Coventry scared Mam. A lorry driver she knew had told her that he had seen bodies hanging from the telephone lines in that city. She was convinced that Nottingham would be next on the list for destruction, even though there was a rumour going around the estate that Lord Haw-Haw, the British traitor and propagandist for Hitler, had promised that Nottingham wouldn't be bombed because the girls who lived there were the prettiest in England. Aunt Mabel was partially consoled by this unlikely story although not with any great faith in its verisimilitude because she still bolted for the shelter, shaking with fear, when the siren went off, which was frequently now. The warning was sounded over 200 times, even though the city was attacked, mercifully, only on 11 occasions.

Mrs Peach and her two children regularly joined us in the Marshall's shelter because she was afraid on her own with her husband, Joe, still on the night shift at the Co-op bakery. When the warning siren drove us out of the house, eight people crammed into the shelter's tight space. We conversed in whispers as though the German airmen in the planes passing overhead might hear us. Joe Peach always raced home from the bakery on his bike at the onset of the sirens when there was a raid on. We could hear him whistling cheerfully as he crossed his garden, the ack-ack battery blasting angrily over his head. He would push the shelter door open to stumble in the darkness among the tense figures snuggling up to each other as if seeking assurance that all would be well as long as they could touch another human being. For a moment we caught the acrid stink of cordite, a deathly smell that brought the war into the womb-like confines of the shelter. Joe did his best to make us feel safe, believe that the air-raid was routine, no more than a nuisance.

"Everybody okay? It's a nice night – quite mild. I'll just get me breath back, then we'll have a fag." He always lit a cigarette when he was settled. I hated it when he plonked himself next to me. His clothes gave off a strong, unpleasant smell, perhaps of sweat after his exertions on his bike, or perhaps its source was some ingredient from the bakery which contaminated his clothes. Whatever it was, it soured the air inside the shelter, and I resented his non-stop cheerful banter when all I wanted to do was listen to the guns, and catch the drone of German bombers overhead.

One night the air itself seemed to be exploding, so powerful and so rapid was the guns' salvos against the bombers. Even Joe was shaken when he tumbled into the shelter. We could hear the window frames in the houses rattling in their frames in that moment when Joe opened the shelter door. "It's a bad night," he admitted. "The shrapnel's falling like rain."

"You ought to have stopped in the shelter at work, duck," Mrs Peach said, frightened. "You could catch a lump of shrapnel while you're on your bike."

"I'll be okay," he reassured her with a laugh. "I'll borrow a tin hat next time."

It was a long night. Eventually the noise subsided and Joe cycled back to work. The rest of us went into the Marshall's house for a cup of tea. At 4.00am the all-clear sounded. "You can have the day off school," Mam said. There was always something to be grateful for, although the unexpected holiday would mean that I would have more than the usual number of errands to run. I had become the family chief shopper. Mam hated queuing. I waited in line inside the gloomy Co-op. There were two counters, both with their own queue. First I waited at the 'fats' counter for bacon, butter and lard. Then I joined a second queue at another counter for tea, sugar and bread, listening to the dreary complaints of hard-pressed women, but remembering to give our Co-op 'divi' number at the end of each transaction. This was important because it meant Mam could claim a little 'cash-back' once a year. I will carry that number in my head to the end of my days: 73641. It was a relief to get served quickly at the greengrocers, then on I scampered to Preston's the ironmongers, with its heady mixture of paraffin and paint smells, to purchase bundles of firewood before nipping into Purdy's the newsagents for Mam's five Woodbines in a paper packet and, if I could diddle the change, the latest *Dandy* or *Beano*. The shop I least looked forward to visiting was Sam the butcher's because it meant rising at dawn to queue outside, often in the dark, for the meat ration – more often than not, corned beef.

One winter's day I was up before the sparrows, shivering in the freezing bedroom and breathed a hole in the beautiful frost patterns on the inside of the window – a frost that burned if I tried to wipe it clear with my fingers. Fresh snow on the ground told me that I would have a foothold down the slope of Bradfield Road. A clear night of frost meant ice on the pavement, metallic in colour, and treacherous. I could hardly walk on ice, my balance was so poor because of my weak right leg – my inheritance from the half-drunk midwife.

When Sam opened his shop I shuffled forward with the queue of frozen women to shiver in a shop that was scarcely warmer than the street outside. The smell of meat fat and chunks of corned beef jelled into a mixture so strong it stirred my empty stomach. Then fast-handed Sam, toothless and built like a whippet, began to slice a slab of pungent corned beef into wafers right under my nose as I gripped the counter for support. Nausea welled up into my throat. My legs slipped uselessly from under me as the light shrunk to a rapidly disappearing point until it was inside my head. I descended into a comforting mist of women's stockinged legs, light bulbs and sawdust. Indistinct voices called from a great distance, like a radio out in space. It was nice. I felt a bit sick, that's all, but warm and cosy. As my head began to clear I realized that I was lying down in sawdust, and a plaster New Zealand lamb was staring at me. I reached out to touch its imbecile face. The voices grew louder, more distinct. "The poor little bogger's coming round. Take him outside into the air!"

I was lifted up and carried out into the Arctic darkness. Somebody set me down on the shop step, forcing my head between my knees. I stared down into a pool of dog pee. I began to sweat, then I cried because I was suddenly embarrassed by the drama I had created. As I walked home with an over-the-ration slice of corned beef safe in my carrier bag I knew it would win me another day off school, a just reward for being wounded in action.

Chapter 7

The Air-raid

My shopping duties were increased when Aunt Mabel, fearful on her own, came to live with us on Frinton Road. She had her toddler son, Michael, to worry about, too. The arrangement would help Mam financially as well as provide mutual comfort and security. She arrived with her posh bedroom suite, her most treasured possession, and a plump pink eiderdown, settling into the front bedroom – which was immediately placed out of bounds to me. The enlarged family worked well enough together, although I became the victim of my aunt's bad moods, especially if I was reading, an activity she regarded as an excuse for idleness, an inferior use of time compared to more constructive activities such as washing-up or fetching the coal in. Having lost Dad as a figure of authority, I thought I would have more freedom to do as I liked. But Mam and Aunt Mabel together more than made up for Dad's absence. Brenda, too, was developing her own powers of criticism, reporting back to Mam when my behaviour was less than perfect, which was often. Sometimes her complaints were justified. One of my more spiteful tricks was to lock her in the pantry or the bathroom when Mam and Aunt Mabel were out – an act of spite she resented for years, with just cause. I defended myself from Aunt Mabel's attacks by "answering back", a rebellious response to her orders which drove her into an incoherent rage, and often cost me a slap from Mam.

Most of the time, fortunately, she was her usual, amiable self, funny and friendly, calling me by my family pet-name: "Del" and treating me to the pictures when I was stony broke. When I disobeyed her I was "a leary sod"; when I ran an errand for her or looked after

Michael, I was "Del" again, and the harmony of the extended family re-established. Nevertheless, I escaped into the streets and into the fields to get away from this regime of bossy women whenever I could, only to return to a double fusilade of wrath at my muddy, unkempt state of dress as I crept in, guiltily, from a hectic mock battle fought on hands and knees through one of the abandoned building sites.

It was Aunt Mabel who denied me the dramatic climax of the only occasion I actually saw a German raider. Uncannily, the action began like my first experience of war: the daytime air-raid in the rain that had been a false alarm. It was lunchtime, and raining, a heavy downpour in late spring, sudden, drenching, and brief. I was soaked as I ran home from school, my shoes clinging squelchingly to my feet like wet cardboard. Mam wouldn't believe that I hadn't been splashing through puddles, in spite of my considering such infantile pleasures as beneath me now that I was nine years old. My shoes, socks and jacket were drying before the fire while I hurried through my dinner, smarting at Mam's suspicions as to how I had got so wet, when the warning siren wailed, followed almost at once by the Bilborough guns opening up in a ferocious battering of the air above the house. The windows and doors were rattling as though a manic wind was trying to force its way in. Aunt Mabel screamed, yanked Michael from the table – his yell of protest at being so forcibly removed from his dinner adding to the chaos – and ran for the back door. Brenda, usually so calm, began to cry.

"Get down the shelter!" Mam shouted. "Never mind your shoes!"

We ran, Brenda and I in bare feet, through the kitchen, dived through the fence and took a short cut over Mr Marshall's seedbeds. Aunt Mabel, perhaps a little ashamed of beating us children to the shelter, allowed us to pass her. I glanced up at the sky before I entered the shelter. Above our heads was a German, twin-engined plane low enough for me to make out the black-cross insignia on its wings. Following it as it raced beneath the clouds were fluffy-looking balls of black-grey flak smoke which seemed to appear magically as each shell burst. My first sight of the enemy! The closest I had ever been to Adolf Hitler. I was thrilled, fascinated. It was like watching a scene from a film being played out on the screen of the sky. It was happening before my eyes, yet the distance turned it into a fiction no nearer to my life than a war film at the Forum Cinema. As I stared up at the dark, twin engined plane hurtling through the flak smoke I was disturbed by the thought that there were men in that machine. If the plane was hit, they would probably be killed. The fact that they were Germans who flew over our town to kill *us* seemed irrelevant. I wanted to see the plane hit by one of the shells, yet I wanted the men to be saved. At the doorway of the shelter I hung back, absorbed by the plane, and puzzled by the confusion of my thoughts. Then there was a breath-stopping blast from the guns which seemed to crack the air above us. Aunt Mabel screamed, Michael hanging on to her neck, as she thumped me in the back to send me flying into the shelter. The sound of the guns died away leaving behind an eerie silence which was broken, finally, by the grizzling of my brother, Peter, and Michael, who always did things together. After the all-clear sounded a few minutes later we all trooped back into the house under a cloudy but peaceful sky, the thin wisps of flak smoke drifting away.

Back at school, fact became lost in fanciful rumour so that the truth of the outcome was never certain. A classmate claimed that the plane had been brought down. One boy reported that he had seen its death dive, although we didn't believe him. Somebody else said that he'd seen parachutes open, and that the plane had crashed ten miles away. What was certain was that the plane was a solitary raider which had flown at roof-top height over the eastern suburbs of the city, machine-gunning the streets as well as a school playground. What puzzled me was why a crew would fly to the middle of England in daylight, and so dangerously low. It seemed an act of blind hate, or perhaps of madness, a crazy last flight by men who had reached the limit of their endurance. Perhaps there was a simpler, military solution, a reconnaissance flight perhaps. I knew that what those airmen had done was evil, but I still felt some sort of compassion for them. They were men and far from home. Their destruction would be real, and no mere flicker of images on the screen of a picture house. The same reality could be waiting for Dad, Uncle Herbert, and Cousin Tommy. The war was more serious than I had imagined. It was no game, no spectacle, no source of second-hand excitement featuring Errol Flynn or Clark Gable. That image of that dark, thrusting shape racing in desperation through murderous flak haunted me for years.

May, 1941, developed into the most destructive period of the war for Nottingham. On the night of May 8th and the morning of May 9th, nearly a hundred German bombers droned over the city, some of their bombs dropping harmlessly in the rural Vale of Belvoir, fifteen miles away. But many fell in what seemed random brutality on the eastern and southern suburbs, as well as on the city centre itself. A cellar under a factory, used by families in the street, received a direct hit which killed all the occupants, most of them women and children. Many years later I was to work in that same factory. We ate our lunchtime sandwiches facing the rough brick wall that separated us from the cellar that had become a grave. We knew what had once lain behind the wall, but no one spoke of it, although we avoided being down there on our own. In Nottingham, there were 40 major fires; 200 houses were destroyed, another 200 were badly damaged. The rest centres gave succour to 1,286 people who had been made homeless. Over 150 people were killed, some of them in their homes in quiet residential areas, lulled into a fatal complacency. After all, was it likely that a German bomb would find an unregarded semi-detached in a city of factories, railyards and workshops?

The worst night of the Nottingham "blitz" began like so many before it. So routine had the warning siren become that Mam kept us up to wait for it. Peter and Michael were oblivious in warm sleep on the settee as Brenda and I talked desultarily in front of the fire. Aunt Mabel was on edge, constantly fussing from the kitchen to the living-room and back again, picking up Michael's clothes to fold, then returning to fold them once more. Mam watched her, lighting cigarette after cigarette, perhaps to divert her mind from dwelling on the prospect of another night of wakeful anxiety. When we crawled sleepily to the Marshall's shelter, before the wail of the siren had died away, there was little indication that this warning signified anything other than one more dreary, cold and uncomfortable period of waiting for the all-clear to sound. The cloudless sky looked innocent with just one or two searchlights sweeping across it. Ack-ack guns echoed eerily from a distant part of the city, the Bilborough guns silent, as though poised for their moment.

Mrs Peach joined us carrying Rodney, her toddler son, while her sister nursed the younger daughter. Like Aunt Mabel, the sister had sought the companionship of a shared house because her husband was away in the army. I anticipated the arrival of a whistling Joe Peach, and wasn't looking forward to it. Suddenly the Bilborough guns roared into action, accompanied by another sound, that of planes. I was fully awake, now, and concentrating on the odd rhythm of what I guessed to be German bombers. This, I thought, was no solitary raider, but a genuine air-raid, a whole sky of Germans carrying bombs. I wondered if they were Dorniers, Heinkel's or Junkers. If I hadn't been so scared I might have tried to sneak out of the shelter to look. But that was impossible, anyway. Their strange, low throbbing engines were threatening and intrusive, growing louder so that I could hear them even above the guns. Aunt Mabel was squirming in agitation, waking a grump Michael as a result. "Hark at them, our Ada. They're right over our heads!" she said staring up at the ceiling of the shelter as if she thought the Germans were flying a few feet above it.

Mr Marshall was with us that night, trying his best to calm the women. "It'll be alright," he said uncertainly. "They'll be on their way to the Rolls Royce factory at Derby. There's nothing in Nottingham for them."

Even I knew that wasn't true, but white lies were consoling, familiar voices a safety net you could cling to. But Mam denied Aunt Mabel the affirmation that all was well in spite of the danger, perhaps because she was weary. "They could be after the gun factory," she remarked as though lost in thought. The factory was an ordinance depot no more than four miles away. Aunt Mabel gave a little moan and squeezed the restless Michael, making him wriggle and complain at being held so tightly.

"I hope Joe doesn't bike home," Mrs Peach said, also affected by the tactless guess at the bombers' destination. The gun factory was only half a mile away from the Co-op bakery. "I hope he goes down the shelter, this time." There was genuine fear in her voice.

I was listening to the orchestration of explosions in the distance. There was something different in the sound. Then I *felt* the difference, and it was like an electric shock. Counterpointing the distinctive crack of the ack-ack shells bursting was a duller "thump" that sent the softest tremor through the soles of my feet and through the post of the bunk bed I was clutching so tightly. The "thumps" came not through the air, but seemed to travel underground as though they were detonations deep in the earth. They were bombs exploding. I knew it, and blurted it out.

"Listen!" I shouted. "The Jerries are dropping bombs!"

"Shurrup our Del!" Aunt Mabel cried, perhaps hoping I was merely teasing her.

"They are!" I insisted, ignoring the warning glare from Mam. "Listen, you can hear them. You can feel the vibration."

We all listened. I was holding my breath. The weak detonations were far away, yet the realization that Nottingham was being bombed froze us into a numbed, unbelieving silence disturbed only by the fretful whimpering of Michael.

"They're a long way off," Mr Marshall said at last. "You could be right, Ada. It could be the gun factory getting a packet."

We sat hunched on the edge of our bunks, listening to the echoes of destruction travelling from somewhere in the east of the city. "I hope Joe's not on his bike in this," Mrs Peach said, "I hope he's got more sense." Somehow, the thought of Joe on his bike released the tension. "I hope he's borrowed a tin hat," her sister said, and we all laughed at the image of Joe puffing and peddling up Aspley Lane with a warden's tin hat on his head.

My thoughts ran in their usual way, like a newsreel or a shot from a movie: limp bodies were being lifted by grim-faced rescue men from the shattered brick and timber that had once been a house. The occupants had been transformed into rag dolls, lolling arms and legs covered in dust and blood. Surely that couldn't happen to me? People as insignificant as me didn't get killed so dramatically – that was for other people, the ones God chose. He wouldn't choose me because I wasn't important enough. He wouldn't bother. I listened to the raid going on in the distance as though it was a game played by strangers in a part of the city I had never seen, and my confidence that I wouldn't be a victim of the war returned. It was too fantastic that a bomb from Berlin in Germany should fall on number twenty-eight Frinton Road, Broxtowe Estate, England, and the fantastic never happened – that was strictly reserved for daydreams, those secret adventures in the mind.

Measurable time ceased to have meaning in such a tense suspension of reality. How long did we sit in silence, listening? A minute? An hour? I don't know. It lasted for ever, then it was finished and we were ourselves again. The sound of the Bilborough guns died away, leaving a space for our lives to resume. A shouted greeting from two of the loudest neighbours across the gardens was confirmation that the mundane had survived, was still going on, and we were grateful.

"Have yo bin alright, Hilda?"

"I've bin alright, Nell. Have you?"

"It's bin a bogger, ent it?"

"It gets on yer bleddy nerves."

"See you later, Ta-ra!"

Somebody's mongrel yelped in protest at these voices in the darkness, but we all laughed. The familiar was a balm to a fear that had been new, shocking and unreal. Becoming a hero was going to be more difficult than Errol Flynn made it appear up there on the screen of the Forum. Guns banged away intermittently for a while, perhaps in the Derby area, then the all-clear came and we all crawled out of the shelter in the hour before dawn. Joe Peach hadn't turned up, and we all thought he must have taken refuge in the bakery air-raid shelter. Mrs needed Mam to tell her over and over again that Joe would have spent the night in the shelter with his workmates. "You'll see, he'll roll up soon. I bet he's on his bike now."

"I shan't go to bed," Mrs Peach said. She was cradling her sleeping daughter in her arms while her sister carried the older child. "I shall wait up for him."

"You want to get some sleep, duck," Mam said. "He'll expect to find you all in bed when he gets home."

"I'm past sleep. I'm frightened, Ada. I've got a funny feeling about it."

The anxiety and fatigue conveyed by Mrs Peach's voice in the darkness of the garden was a sign that she could not be placated by words anymore. She turned to squeeze through the gap in the fence that Joe had made for her.

Aunt Mabel was too shaken to return to her bed. "I daren't go upstairs. They'll only come back again if I do. Stop with us, Ada," she pleaded.

We stayed up for nearly an hour drinking tea, ears cocked for any sound, however faint, that might be an overture to the bombers' return. At last, Mam, exhausted herself by her efforts to calm her sister and Mrs Peach, finally succumbed to her weariness and drove us, stumbling, to our beds.

* * *

Sleep was warm, consoling, the soft breathing of Peter snuggling close to me was safe and reassuring. But the urgent knocking on the back door dragged me back to the bare bedroom. I could hear Mam from her bedroom grumbling as she got dressed. She shouted for me to go down to see who was creating such a disturbance. Half-asleep, I put on my trousers and shirt, padded dozily down the stairs. I glanced at the clock in the living room. It was seven a.m. We had been in bed only three hours. The knocking continued as I slid the bolt and yanked the back-door open. Mrs Peach stood in the porch. She was crying, her eyes red with exhaustion, her face swollen and ugly.

"Tell your Mam I want her," she said.

Mam came into the kitchen before I could turn to fetch her. Before either could speak, Mrs Peach let out a wrenching sob from deep inside her chest.

"What's the matter? What's wrong?" Mam put her arm around Mrs Peach's waist and helped her into the kitchen, setting her down heavily into a chair. She probably guessed what was wrong, and I, too, realized something must have happened to Joe. Mam ordered me into the living room to make the fire, no doubt to save me the embarrassment of witnessing the sight of a grieving woman.

I drew back the curtains, screwed up last night's *Evening Post* into a ball, placed sticks, which had been left in the hearth, over the paper, then realized that I would have to go back into the kitchen to fetch the coal. I retrieved small pieces of coke from the grate and managed to get a new fire started. I couldn't make out what Mrs Peach was saying. Her voice was too low, too thick and broken to decipher. I sat on the floor in front of the struggling flames, and waited. At last, I heard the back door close. I went into the kitchen to fetch coal. Mam was outside helping Mrs Peach through the gap in the fence.

"What's up." I asked when she came back. The strain on her face frightened me a little. I'd never seen her looking so vulnerable before.

"The Co-op bakery's been bombed. They hit the air-raid shelter," Mam said, her face white. "They think Joe's been killed."

At ten o'clock, Mrs Peach's sister came to the back door. She, too, had been crying.

"Will you look after the kids, Ada. We've got to go to the bakery. A policeman's taking us."

That seemed to confirm that Joe was dead. Mam tried to hide the details of the tragedy from Brenda and me, but I was always listening to what adults were saying, whether they knew it or not. Now I was awestruck by the fact that I knew someone who had been killed in the war, but found it hard to imagine cheerful, whistling Joe as dead. Death was too remote, like an event to which children are not admitted, something which went on, mysteriously, behind closed doors. Joe Peach had gone into the shelter under the bakery because bombs were dropping close by. One hit the bakery, and the floors above the shelter collapsed into it, the heavy machinery crushing most of the occupants. A workmate remembered Joe telling him: "I'll just have a fag in the shelter while this lot's on, then I'll get off home." They were his last words.

All the rescue workers found of Joe was a foot, recognized by Mrs Peach because of the blue sock still on it. Perhaps remembering him now after so many years is my atonement for the inadequacy of my feelings, then. And for my shame at remembering, at the time, how much I hated the smell of his workman's clothes.

Chapter 8

The French-Canadian

Uncle George Kew surprised the family by suddenly announcing that he had volunteered for the Pioneer Corps. It wasn't because he was particularly patriotic, in fact he was just as likely to declare war against the British Army as against Rommel if he had a mind to. Perhaps the spirit of daring which drove him to volunteer for service as an under-age soldier in the Great War lived in him still. After the challenge of Broxtowe Wood had been satisfied, he had taken up with a gang of rabbit poachers for a time, a nocturnal adventure that he enjoyed until they were chased by gamekeepers one night. They had escaped from a wood, and had taken refuge in the back of a pal's lorry at the last second. One of the gang had fallen off the tail-board still clutching his booty. When his friend was hauled before the magistrate and heavily fined, Uncle George lost interest in illicit rodents and looked around for some other means to express his considerable energy. Joining the army must have seemed suitable because it was legal, and everybody else was doing it, although it came as a great shock to Aunt Liz.

The consequence of his rashness was that Aunt Liz and Cousin Ida moved in to live with us on Frinton Road, thus increasing the figures of female authority to three adults, and two enthusiastic trainees in Brenda and Ida. Separately, and in their own homes, Aunt Liz and Aunt Mabel were welcoming, even affectionate towards me. But having me under their feet all day seemed to get on their nerves. I was nagged in relays. Perhaps my aunts saw something in me that must have reminded them of Dad, an off-hand independence and cheekiness which they interpreted as arrogance, which was one of his

53

chief failings in their eyes. I tried to make myself scarce by reading books to escape their attention, but this only made matters worse as they regarded reading mere "lounging about", an act of bone idleness. Neither could my aunts understand Mam's laxness in allowing me to stay out in the street after dark without reporting where I was going, what I was going to do when I got there, and who I was going to do it with. If I came in after nine o'clock at night, usually unkempt with grubby hands, knees and face, it was my aunts who complained. Mam thought that a curt order to "get washed and up to bed" was sufficient punishment, knowing that I loved to stay up late, while my aunts considered being scruffy *and* late was a "pasting" offence.

Brenda enjoyed my ordeal, and was always on the side of our aunts. Young as she was, my sister had come to the conclusion that I was vain, disrespectful, as well as spiteful. She agreed with our aunts that I deserved to be "taken down a peg or two." She was probably right, being a sound judge of character for one so young. Sometimes she stirred up trouble for me, especially if I'd behaved particularly badly towards her. She reported my misdemeanours, or my sins of omission, especially of domestic duties, in an appropriate dramatic tone of voice: "He locked me in the pantry again when you was out. He threw the dirty washing all over the kitchen floor so *I* would have to pick it up. Mrs Marshall had to shout at him to make less noise. And I saw him with that Ernie, who smokes. There was some girls with them. He never washed the pots like you told him. *I* had to do them!"

My only ally against this barrage of truth was my cousin, Ida. Her good humour often diverted her mother's concern for my moral welfare, lifting the mood by asking if anybody fancied a cup of tea, a certain method of improving the attitude of the family of women, who could never resist a fresh pot of tea. Ida laughed off Brenda's condemnation of my weakness and vanity. "Leave him alone – he's a lad isn't he? All lads are daft!"

Relief from the ordeals of the day lay in being left in Ida's care when Mam and her sisters put on their best two-piece or a frock, painted their legs with simulated stocking liquid, or sand mixed with water if it had run out, then toddled off to the Beacon for a beer and a sing-song without a husband in sight. At last, Mam's Angel of Luck was smiling on her for a while. She and Aunt Mabel had jobs at the Raleigh Cycle factory as machinists, turning out .303 bullets on piece work, repetitive labour which gave them fat pay packets on a Friday night. Mam had never known such prosperity. Dad was a peaceful distance away learning to drive a tank in Scarborough. Uncle Herbert was closer to home, being stationed fifteen miles away in Derby, while Uncle George Kew was pioneering somewhere. The sisters were free, and if not exactly independent they at least had money to spend on themselves in the style of their days as single girls. If the warning siren went off while they were in the pub, they would hurry home, dashing into the living room puffing and panting, complaining that they had left half-finished glasses of mild beer even though the threatened air-raid didn't materialise, and their evening was ruined.

Brenda and I were allowed to stay up with Ida until our mothers returned. She entertained us with her repertoire of sad ballads and stories of dying orphans, babies, mothers, fathers and grandparents. These epics of general woe were intended to show us how lucky we were in having living, breathing relatives when so many families were losing theirs. Usually, Brenda fell asleep under the narcotic effect of Ida's depressing tales, but I fought leaden eyelids against missing the return of Mam and my aunts, anticipating their good humour – if the sirens hadn't gone off to spoil it. Aunt Liz and Aunt Mabel treated me with beery camaraderie on such occasions, even if they had been nagging me remorselessly all day.

On Saturday nights they would burst into the house singing their favourite songs such as *One Of These Days*, which Aunt Mabel rendered with the passion of Sophie Tucker, if not with the art, while Mam preferred *South Of The Border* or the lugubrious *Carolina Moon*. Sometimes they would be accompanied by newly made friends from the pub, women on their own, or with their husbands carrying bulbous bottles of Nut Brown ale. Then the beer would be poured into cups and mugs because we were short on glasses, a bit of bread and cheese might be shared if the ration would run to it. After the scant supper it would be time for the songs, the sad ones, mostly, for weren't the husbands of the house locked in a barracks far away? And wasn't it lonely on a Saturday night if you lived with your sisters and there were five children to share? I had never seen Mam enjoy herself so much. Nor did she ever enjoy herself so much again.

One night, Mam and Aunt Mabel arrived home soberly with a couple of soldiers, probably family men themselves, for they looked older than Dad. The occasion was very proper: there was no sing-song and, after a drink poured from bottles carried home from the pub, the soldiers disappeared quietly into the night when Mam and Aunt Mabel had thanked them for being so considerate as to walk them home through the blackout. Innocent as it appeared, I was shocked by Mam talking to another man. And what if Dad came home on leave at that moment, unexpectedly? It didn't seem possible that she could have an interest in anyone other than Dad, Brenda, Peter and me. I had assumed that her whole life was dedicated to our welfare. Talking to a stranger, laughing with him, somehow made our world seem less secure.

The good times didn't stop when Uncle Herbert and Uncle George came on leave. Both seemed to get home more often than Dad. Uncle Herbert wangled a pass most weekends. With her husband close at hand, Aunt Mabel would be on her best Sophie Tucker form as she brassily performed, *One of these days, you're gonna miss me, honey. One of these days, you'll be so lonely* – with Uncle Herbert laughing benignly at her antics because she did a suggestive little dance to the old torch song, and her torch for her husband was still burning brightly, fuelled by Shipstone's best mild beer.

Uncle George, too, was not one to miss out on a party, though his stony face never expressed his enjoyment. Being indifferent to military regulation, he arranged his own leaves. Once he was home he stayed until he had run out of money, then returned for his punishment. I also enjoyed his leaves – which were a surprise to Aunt Liz as much as they were to his C.O. The source of my pleasure was the Lee Enfield rifle he usually brought home with him, probably without permission. When the adults were out, I played with it, alarmed by its weight and awkwardness. How did soldiers manage to hold it steady for accurate firing? We would never win the war with guns as unwieldy as the Lee Enfield. It felt like a plank. My favourite game was to take imaginary sniper shots from the living-room window at passing neighbours.

Bang! Down goes Misery Baxter with one in the chest. Crack! Snobby Mrs Hancock gets one in the leg. But the bolt was impossible. I could hardly move it. Grandad Buttress had told me that the British soldiers in the Great War fired their rifles so rapidly the Germans thought they were armed with machine guns. Handling the weapon made that account seem like fantasy.

The rifle was not the only thing Uncle George brought home. One Friday night he turned up with a French-Canadian out of his platoon. He was small and wiry, like Uncle George, but had a dark, foreign face and a mysterious accent that suggested he didn't speak English very often. We all felt sorry for him – he looked so forlorn, out of place. Mam and my aunts were particularly solicitous towards him, feeding and fussing him like a stray that had followed Uncle George home. My uncle acted as interpreter as he seemed to understand his new-found mate's accent without difficulty.

"Ask him if he wants to come for a drink down the Beacon with us," Aunt Liz instructed her husband.

"Of course he wants to come. We aren't leaving him here on his own!"

"He might not drink," Aunt Liz insisted.

"Of course he drinks. What d'you think he is, a bleddy parson?"

The French-Canadian's face lit up. "Thank you very much. I go for drink with you."

Soon the crowd of them departed in high spirits, the family primed to show their foreign guest what a good time could be had on a Friday night down at the Beacon.

He was an exotic visitor in my eyes, a true foreigner, the first I had ever met. He had smiled and nodded to me, an acknowledgement of my existence which made me warm to him. I didn't know what a French-Canadian was, nor why he didn't speak in the soft drawl of the Canadian soldiers who were camped in Bilborough village, and on the pasture we called Strelley Park. They had quickly become accepted as interesting additions to the local scenery, faintly glamorous in spite of their British khaki uniforms. They were popular with the kids of Broxtowe Estate. We begged for badges and buttons at the camp gates. No doubt we were nuisances, but they were patient with us. I learned from Mam and Aunt Mabel that they were a lively bunch at the Beacon, but well behaved, and bought drinks for the locals thereby earning instant acceptance.

* * *

I was dozing in the armchair when I heard the door open. The family had returned from the Beacon later than usual. I had finally succumbed to the drowsiness I disguised from Ida so that she wouldn't bundle me off to bed and miss whatever fun was going. But Mam and my aunts were subdued, serious looking, and I was disappointed.

"It's time you were in bed," Mam said, automatically. She seemed to be thinking about something else.

"Where's Uncle George?" I asked.

No-one answered me. Mam went into the kitchen to put the kettle on. Aunt Liz gave a little moan as she wrenched her court shoes off. Then Uncle George came in, looking somewhat dishevelled. He glanced at me. "It's a bit late for him to be up, isn't it?" Aunt Liz slumped back in her chair with the little moan-come-sigh she always gave when the world had gone awry. "What a palaver," she said. "What a bleddy palaver."

"Give it a rest," Uncle George said. He sounded thoroughly fed up.

"You shouldn't've brought him," Aunt Liz complained. "You never know where you are with foreigners."

Mam came in with the teapot. "The poor little sod," she said, and with such sadness I thought the French-Canadian was dead.

Aunt Mabel hadn't spoken. She sat at the table, pale, obviously frightened by whatever it was that had happened. There was a large damp patch staining the bodice of her frock. They had forgotten about me as I pressed myself deeper into the armchair, taking note of their intriguing conversation. Ida had crept upstairs when she saw that her mother was in a black mood. Brenda had gone to bed an hour before. "I hate this war," Aunt Mabel said at last. "I rotten well hate it!"

It wasn't until the next morning that I managed to piece together what had happened to the quiet soldier. The family had been enjoying themselves in the assembly room of the Beacon. The piano was banging away and the songs were hitting the ceiling. After a while they noticed how morose the little French-Canadian grew as he downed pint after pint. Mam thought he was homesick, and the songs only made his loneliness worse. That night the place was packed with Canadians from the Strelley camp, and they too were in full voice, trying to bridge the enormous distance between home and their tented camp in a Nottingham field.

Then something exploded in the French-Canadian's brain, some deep-set anger surfacing with a shocking suddenness. He leapt to his feet, sweeping beer-filled glasses off their table and, screaming, picked up a chair to attack the Canadians crowding the bar, crashing it over their heads before they had time to duck. He staggered across the room, lurching into tables, beer swilling into people's laps, only to return to the bar where he launched himself into the crowd of Canadians, fists flying.

After the initial paralysis brought on by the suddenness of the attack, the Canadians came to, punching and kicking the little soldier as he went down. The Beacon customers fled for the door, some of them screaming. I never learned how badly he was hurt, or what happened after he was carried out to a police van, apparently unconscious. Uncle George returned to camp the next day, and none of the family ever mentioned the French-Canadian again.

No-one understood why he had attacked his compatriots, or even knew if they were the sole cause of his act of lunacy. The war had exposed us to a wider world beyond the self-regarding, comparatively peaceful island that was Broxtowe Estate. In the light of such foreign behaviour displayed by the French-Canadian, the estate seemed safe and orderly, a haven against the chaos of a war which took husbands away, killed neighbours, and made sad little soldiers mad. A sing-song kept it at bay for a while. It was a way for Mam and my aunts to forget, however briefly, what they hated about the war. They were enjoying a time of affluence and an unwanted freedom. But they knew such things were transitory, of no value when the cost was a world they knew, and trusted.

Chapter 9

The Last Party

The singing didn't stop when Dad first came home on leave. He surprised me by the passive way he followed the Radford family down to the Beacon, returning in quiet good humour as though he was actually enjoying himself in the company of Uncle Herbert and Uncle George. It was so unlike his usual behaviour that I knew it couldn't last. When Cousin Tommy came home on leave to join his mother at our house, followed the next day by Dad, their antagonism towards each other immediately surfaced. My cousin was sitting at the table in Dad's chair, looking very comfortable, a leary smirk on his face. Dad hadn't even taken his coat off when he ordered Tommy out of the house with tight-lipped venom. "Let's see you put me out," Tommy laughed. But we knew he was itching for a fight. "If I go out, you're coming with me."

Aunt Liz came to the rescue for Mam's sake, although she probably saved Dad from a good hiding at the same time. Tommy disappeared, with his kit-bag on his shoulder, to lodge for the week with his aunt in Hyson Green and an uneasy truce between Dad and the Radford clan was established.

The skirmish was the prologue to a bigger row to come, though. Tommy was one Radford too many for Dad, and he was quiet, always a sign of a rising temper. Mam knew that it wouldn't take much for his fuse to blow, and kept out of his way as much as she could. I also sensed the rise in temperature, and tried not to catch Dad's eye, feeling the tension as a slight ache in my stomach. It was Saturday, and the evening after a session down at the Beacon would be the most likely time for the shouting to start.

That night the crowd that followed the family into our living-room was the biggest I had seen. This gave me some comfort. Surely Dad, who hated drawing attention to himself, wouldn't be drawn into a row with such a large audience watching? The men were carrying quart bottles of Nut Brown, the women clutching smaller bottles of pale ale to their bosoms. The table was soon loaded with booze while Mam and Aunt Mabel hunted for mugs, cups and glasses in the kitchen, the babble of beery humour rising in the expectation of a continuing good time. Dad was talking quietly to Uncle Herbert, nodding and weakly smiling in response to my uncle's cheerful banter. But I saw the cold blue distance in his eyes, the unfocussed stare that meant his mind was elsewhere, the anger simmering behind his apparent vacancy. I guessed that an evening in the pub hadn't eased the tension between him and Mam. He never looked at her as she bustled in and out of the room, and she hadn't spoken to him since they came home. I took it as an ominous sign, although everybody else, most of whom were strangers to me, seemed unaware that their hosts were involved in the preliminaries for a big fight.

The women had claimed the few chairs at the table. The men leaned on the sideboard as though it was a bar. Every comment brought a shriek of laughter from the women. I couldn't see anything funny in what they said, or pick out any specific thread of conversation or sense, perhaps because there wasn't one, but only a determination to laugh at anything anybody said because this was a party, and it didn't matter what you laughed at because that's what you did at parties, especially when the sirens might go at any moment.

Dad finally looked across at me crouching in an armchair, peering over the arm in the hope that I wouldn't be noticed. "Do you know what time it is?" he said brusquely. "Come on – let's have you in kip." Protesting vainly at having to miss such a show of adult levity, I was sent to bed fussed over by the half-drunk strangers, the women planting wet, beer-scented kisses on me as I wormed my way to the door.

Climbing into bed at the side of a sleeping Peter, I wondered at the chorus of laughter that suddenly burst from downstairs, subsided for a few seconds then burst out again. I couldn't make out what people were shouting, or what was provoking such ribald hilarity. My curiosity prevented sleep, and when the laughter and shouting eased into a sing-song I hummed along with the familiar tunes of the day. Aunt Mabel did a solo with *One Of These Days* in her most raucous voice, which made Sophie Tucker's vaudeville version sound refined. It earned her shouts of approval and applause. Then Mam started up with *We'll Meet Again*, the rest of the crowd joining in its mournful chorus. After a few more songs the noise drifted into conversation, then into silence. Perhaps they were topping up their mugs and their glasses prior to another bout of singing. But I was too tired to wait, and drifted into sleep.

How long I slept, I don't know. It seemed like only seconds before I was jolted awake by a thumping noise, then a burst of laughter, prolonged and accompanied by whooping shouts. There was another "thump", as though somebody was kicking the wall downstairs. Whatever was happening seemed to be considered hysterically funny judging by the unconstrained shrieks which accompanied the "thumps". They were loud enough to make Peter stir and grumble in his sleep. I eased myself out of bed, fully awake now, then crept downstairs.

Opening the hall door quietly, I peeped into the living-room. It was hard to focus immediately, there were so many people crowding it. Then I saw Aunt Mabel, and she was upside down. Her frock was tucked into her knickers as she did a handstand against the wall by the window, her stockinged feet planted firmly on the flower patterned wallpaper, her chubby arms wobbling under her weight. I was acutely embarrassed – even more so when I realized that most of the women had tucked their skirts into their knickers the way young girls did when they practised handstands against a street wall. Mam was waiting her turn in this state of dishevillment, my embarrassment turning to shock when I saw her.

Suddenly I was spotted. A woman shouted, "Look at the lad nosing!" and laughed. All eyes turned towards me and missed seeing Aunt Mabel's arms collapse, sending her sliding down the wall in a heap of fat legs and arms to finish in a heap on the floor. I tore back upstairs, diving into bed, my heart racing. I was ashamed of what I had witnessed. How could I look Mam in the face again? How could she and Aunt Mabel act so stupidly in front of all those strangers? Brenda would never believe me in the morning when I reported what I had seen. I steamed in priggish anger until Dad called up the stairs, a hard-toned restraint in his voice telling me that he was trying to control his own anger. "Stay in your bed, don't come down again. It's nearly twelve o'clock. Get to sleep."

"It's too noisy!" I shouted back, resentful.

"Do as I say. Get some kip! They're going now."

After he had closed the hall door I heard only an indistinct hum of conversation, low and strangely soothing. Soon I was lulled into another sleep, the image of Aunt Mabel's clumsy gymnastics fading into dreams.

I must have reached a more profound level of sleep this time, because the noise which dragged me out of it seemed like part of a dream that lingered for a moment into wakefulness, as dreams and nightmares sometimes do. But this was no dream. The noise from downstairs was different, rising up in a frightening cacophony of anger. Mostly, it was Dad's voice shouting, the language violently punctuated by bangs which I knew would be his fist striking the table. There were other voices, too, placating, pleading, and Mam's voice rising to a shout that was almost a scream. I lay in fear, my nerves so taut that I couldn't move even if I wanted to. I had lain like this before as their raging tempers flared into arguments below. But this was the worst row between them that I had ever heard. It terrified me by its intensity. I longed for the oblivion of sleep again, closing my eyes tightly as though it would come that way. But such a wish was futile. The brooding anger of Dad since the altercation with Tommy had burst out, possessing him, so unrelenting was his shouting, so vicious was its tone. Mam was shouting back, her voice choked as though she was crying. It was impossible to make out what was being said, nor did I want to know. I simply wanted it to stop. I pulled the covers over my head in a vain attempt to shut out the angry voices. But there was nowhere to hide from the sheer physical pain that hurt my stomach and squeezed my chest.

When I heard the hall door yanked open I thought that the pair of them were about to carry the argument into one of the bedrooms.

Mam came up the stairs alone. She was crying as she entered my bedroom, deep seated sobs making her catch her breath. She was still for a few moments, as if she were listening, perhaps trying to detect whether I was asleep or not, then she sat on my bed. I heard footsteps on the stairs, and I held my breath, wondering if it was Dad. A woman entered my room, one of the strangers. Mam had slumped onto the edge of my bed. Through half-closed eyes I could make out her figure. She touched my shoulder, then leaned over me to touch Peter as if making sure we were there in the darkness. I lay perfectly still, feigning sleep, not daring to ask why she was crying or what had provoked Dad's anger to a pitch that terrified me.

"Don't get upset, duck," the stranger said quietly, as though she was trying to calm a child.

"It's only my kids I live for," Mam choked. Somehow her words sounded too melodramatic, a line from a bad film at the Forum, or one of those dramatic pronouncements that you heard on the bus when the crowd from the Beacon shouted to each other when they'd had one too many. Even as very small kids we thought beer talk was funny.

"That's right," the stranger said. She sounded kind, one of the women I saw patiently counting pennies out of her purse in the Co-op queue. "Think about your kids. You've got to keep going for them ent you?"

"My kids are all I care about," Mam repeated. "It's only them as keeps me here."

"That's right," the stranger repeated. "Don't let him upset you like this. He ent worth it."

The voices from the living-room were subdued now. I guessed that the climax of the row had passed. Dad's wild anger would have ebbed into a more restrained channel of bitterness, as it always did. The pattern was familiar to me: first he would shout, a potential physical violence spent in striking the table with his fist. This would be followed by a tenseness that would strangle his words so that he could hardly speak. Finally there would be a brooding silence, like a clenched fist poised in the air.

In a little while Aunt Liz called up the stairs to the stranger. "Hilda, Stan wants to go now!"

64

The woman called back, giving Mam a few more comforting words before she said her goodnight and plodded back down the stairs. Aunt Liz came into the room when the stranger had gone. "Come on down, Ada," she said, more in the way of an order than a request. "Don't tek any notice of that sod."

"I'm not coming down," Mam said. She seemed more controlled now. "I've had enough of his bleddy games. I'm not taking it any more."

Aunt Liz drew in a deep breath, as though she was at a loss for something consoling to say. "I don't know," she moaned. "I don't know how you bleddy stick him."

"He's rotten," Mam said, her voice thick with phlegm. "He's rotten right through. I wish he'd fall under a bus."

Even Aunt Liz didn't know how to cope with Mam's most despairing moods. "I don't know ... Try to get some sleep, then," she offered helplessly.

The back door opened. Footsteps trailed down the garden path, the low notes of voices fading.

"They're all going," Aunt Liz said. "I'd better get back downstairs." She sounded relieved at the excuse for escape.

The last footsteps died away. From below I could just make out the voices of my aunts, but no sound from Dad. I guessed that they had talked him out of the terrible anger. They didn't look into my room when they came to bed, perhaps thinking it was best to let their sister alone in case her despair touched off another row.

I lay awake for a long time, listening to Mam's breathing as she lay by my side. It was easier now, except for a little shuddering exhalation like that of a child's in the final throes of a tantrum. I was about to doze off myself, thinking that she was truly asleep, when I heard the hall door open and Dad's footsteps on the stairs. He ascended slowly, as though he was weary, then paused on the landing. I thought for a moment he would enter my bedroom, and dreaded it. Mam must have woken, because I felt her body stiffen, then relax as Dad went back downstairs closing the hall door quietly after him.

There were no more parties after that, and the singing stopped for ever. I never really knew what the row was about, understanding only

65

that it was fired by something more powerful than Tommy's presence in the house. I knew only that that fear arising out of what can't be understood has more terror in it than all known fears. What Mam probably understood was that the personal, malevolent star which she believed in so passionately had returned to plague her.

Chapter 10

A Mystery Trip

Alan, my first Broxtowe pal, was a bony lad. He was so thin his kneecaps, elbows and wrists were clearly skeletal. His pale face turned purple in the cold winds blowing from the building site skirting Bradfield Road. A smile from him was wintry, his laugh dry and chesty. It soon became apparent to me that I was the only friend he had. His isolation wasn't because he was rejected by other kids on the estate, but because he was aloof, indifferent, it seemed, to roaming the streets looking for something interesting to do. He was even less interested in *making* something happen, which is how the rest of us spent our leisure time. I enjoyed his company and his surprising humour. We walked home from school together, chatting about the war, about Adolf Hitler and George Formby films which we both loved. Going to the kids' matinee on a Saturday afternoon at the Forum Cinema was his only recreation as far as I could see.

"Are you coming out later?" I would ask as we hurried home from school. Alan wasn't allowed to dawdle.

There would be an embarrassed silence. "I can't. Our mam won't let me 'cos I've got to do the errands and all that."

His "Mam" was his stepmother and, according to Alan, ruled his life with an oppressive discipline. He wasn't allowed to play in the street. If he lingered at his gate talking to me when we reached Frinton Road his stepmother would come to the front door to call him in, glaring with a hostility that puzzled me. So far, I had done nothing to warrant it. Everything Alan did was on the run. He ran all the way down the hill to the shops for his stepmother, and he ran all the way back again, no matter how heavy his load. Sometimes I would see him, purple faced as he scampered from shop to shop, croaking a chesty "Hi-ya" in greeting. In my imagination Alan's stepmother became the epitome of cruelty, on a par with the cruel stepmothers of fairytales. She was the cold negation of motherhood, the storybook stepmother who had transformed her amiable stepson into a harassed running boy. Throughout the war I saw him run, even from friendship. Curious about his secret indoor life I attempted to probe it on our way home from school one day.

"What do you do stuck in the house every night? It'd drive me barmy!"

"I have things to do. I wash the pots and mop the floor and all that. Then I listen to the wireless a bit before I go to bed at nine o'clock."

Such enforced domestic duties seemed to be the worst cruelty of all. I would have rebelled against endless pot washing and floor mopping with the double summer-time sun still out at ten o'clock at night, with Broxtowe Woods, Strelley fields and orchards beckoning. I pitied him for not being part of a gang roaming the streets, sharing the excitement only a gang can generate. What really puzzled me was that Alan didn't seem to mind his lack of freedom too much. He never complained about his treatment, even though I expressed sympathy for his imprisonment. That seemed to embarrass him, and the thought crossed my mind that perhaps he actually *liked* staying in to wash pots and mop floors.

My growing scepticism about his reasons for not being able to join me on the street was reinforced when I became bold enough to knock on his back door, for the first time, to call him out, dare him to leave his washing and swabbing for a game of tennis-ball footie on the street. It was Alan himself who came to the door. He eased it open a few inches so that I had the merest glimpse of an immaculate kitchen with painted brickwork and a shining gas stove. He didn't seem pleased to see me. The sense of being on the edge of something oppressive, a joyless regime dedicated to cleanliness, a life which was witheringly private was heightened by the smell of disinfectant. After a moment or two of teasing persuasion on my part, and an uncharacteristic, surly rejection by Alan, his stepmother emerged from the living-room. A dour, youngish woman, heavily built and wearing thick glasses, she pulled the door open wider. She stared at me, Alan darting behind her as if for protection. "He's not coming out," she said tonelessly. "He doesn't want to. Don't come again." She was obviously irritated that I had disturbed their private world. Then she slammed the door on me.

It would have been easy to match the sour woman who came to the door with Alan's tales about his domineering stepmother, but I wondered if Alan was telling the truth about her. Was it true that he didn't want to come out? I came to the conclusion that he might actually *want* to be on his own. He didn't want friendship, even though we spent time together at school. He must have realised that I thought being a loner was odd. He had concocted his story about being a virtual prisoner in his own house. When, at last, I understood the reason for his lies, his self-imposed isolation seemed an affront to me, a rejection I resented. At school, and on our journeys home, he was relaxed, a cheerful pal who shared a joke. Out of school he became a puzzle to me. Why did he run away as soon as we got to Frinton Road? And why did he run all the time? Run like a scared rabbit straight past me, past the friends he might have shared? Run through his childhood?

The answers were beyond me. Angry because I couldn't find them, I chased him home from school one day after an argument, catching him within a few strides of his front gate and punched him, cutting his lip and gashing my knuckles on his front teeth. It was the end of any possibility of friendship, and I felt deep shame for my act of cruelty.

* * *

The friend I turned to after Alan's rejection was Ernie, a year older than me, a wiry, nerveless lad who lived on Withern Road at the bottom of the hill. He had a mop of tangled waves which he couldn't get a comb through until he tamed them with a dollop of lard. He could shin up a tree or onto a roof like a trained chimp and spot a bird's nest in a Strelley hedge quicker than any of us. In the summer he swam in the muddy canal serving Wollaton pit, thrashing the black water in an ungainly crawl while I watched timidly from the towpath, afraid to trust my weak right leg as a swimmer. One of his greatest pleasures was to smoke discarded cigarette butts he had collected from the gutter or from the floor of the Forum. Nothing we did gave him satisfaction unless there was a risk involved. When we were caught scrumping apples, pears or damsons in the cottage gardens of Strelley village, or were grabbed by the ape-man who guarded the door of the Forum as we tried to sneak in without paying, Ernie would grin, enjoying the excitement, while I burst into shameful tears of panic. He accepted and forgave my weakness in such situations, while I admired his nerve and his defiant cheek. Whenever I got into trouble it was because I had meekly followed Ernie into forbidden territory: an orchard, the roof of the rent office from which we lifted tiles to get at house martins' nests for their eggs. At night we traversed back gardens on the estate in total darkness like marauders searching for booty, although we never found anything worth stealing. The danger was sufficient reward in itself as far as Ernie was concerned when we climbed fences and gates, or tip-toed up garden paths to search for left-out toys or garden implements.

Ernie's relationship with his dad was one I envied. Mr Walker was a wounded veteran of World War One, a stalwart member of the British Legion, coming home from his visits to their club tipsy, and cheerful. He displayed his medals upon his chest whenever an appropriate occasion arose, such as Remembrance Sunday, or King George's birthday. His showy patriotism was strange to me. My Buttress grandad had also been wounded while fighting in the trenches, but he rarely spoke of it, and then only in response to my wonder at his close encounter with death in the infamous Delville Wood. Ernie's dad, though, would take every opportunity to describe in graphic detail the horrors of war, including an account of how his leg was shattered by German machine-gun bullets.

Ernie was so at ease with his dad the two of them were like friends, always affectionate towards each other. Seeing them share a joke made my dad's indifference towards me seem even more hurtful. It was easy to see why Ernie was so confident: Mr Walker, like the rest of his family, didn't bother too much about the world beyond their own front door, the happy-go-lucky mood of the household being set by four dizzy, singing, anarchic daughters, my favourite being Peggy, a vivacious fifteen year old, pretty, and fresh out of a home for wayward girls.

As far as Ernie was concerned, his dad's wry observations on life were the source of all wisdom, especially about the need to be loyal to the King, even unto death, and the sheer luck of being born in England rather than somewhere backward. It was inevitable that Ernie placed patriotism above all else, even above honesty and education – which accounted for his not being able to read or write, and was why he nicked everything that wasn't tied down. Whenever *God Save The King* was played on the wireless, Mr Walker struggled to his feet and wobbled to attention. He performed this rite even if he was having his dinner, or was in the middle of a conversation. If any of his daughters, Dolly, Peggy, Doreen or Shirley dared to giggle while this display of loyalty was taking place, their formidable mother would shut them up immediately. "Shut up you lot! It's the King!" she would proclaim as though George the Sixth had just dropped in for a cup of tea and a biscuit. Scowling at his irreverent sisters, Ernie would throw his head back in line with a stiffened spine, his thumbs straight down the seams of his trousers as demonstrated by the wounded old infantryman, his dad.

As the final notes of the anthem died away, and cheerful dance music returned, Mr Walker gave a stiff-armed salute before flopping back into his chair. The non-stop, often ribald chit-chat of the girls would burst out again counterpointed by the never-ending music from the wireless speaker hanging precariously from the picture rail of the crowded living room. I always sat beneath the speaker, loving the swing of the music, my head joyfully spinning from it, as well as from the chatter of the girls. Their whispered secrets and their puzzling innuendoes were followed by cries of raucous laughter which indicated a mysterious sexuality that seemed far more enticing than Mr Walker's war stories, or learning to salute the national anthem.

Ernie helped his dad to make a living by selling bundles of firewood from a dray which was pulled by a shaggy, defeated looking horse. It was Ernie's job to harness the horse in preparation for the day's round in this low-profit enterprise. When the dray was ready, and loaded, Mr Walker urged the reluctant horse out of the cobbled stableyard which was situated in a side street in Radford. The rig clattered along Alfreton Road, an artery connecting the northern suburbs to the centre of the city, the old horse competing with swerving vans and buses. Sometimes, on school holidays, I went with them. I always felt undignified to be tossed about on the dusty floorboards of the dray as we lurched dangerously round a stationary bus or hit a raised draincover in the road. If I spotted somebody who knew me, I tried to act nonchalant, as though travelling like a gypsy with a load of firewood was a treat denied them.

The only time I really enjoyed a journey on the dray was when Mr Walker decided to use it to take the kids of Withern Road on an excursion. It was to be a "mystery trip", a Whit Monday holiday treat. About twenty of us gathered outside the Walker's house, including Ernie's two younger sisters, and several kids I had never seen before. We set off for the unknown under a perfect sky clutching packets of sandwiches wrapped in newspaper, swigging from bottles of Tizer or lemonade. Twenty pairs of legs dangled over the sides of the dray while the sweating horse toiled and the iron-clad wheels rolled noisily over the back lanes of Strelley. When we skirted fields of deep grass, partridge whirred into the air with an explosive noise that stopped the breath for a second. The shock of it made the girls scream, then laugh because they seemed to enjoy being frightened. A shoal of barrage balloons hung, brilliantly silver, in the distance. Even the horse picked up speed as if it was responding to the shrill laughter and excitement behind him, breaking into a dangerous gallop which rocked the dray, Mr Walker fighting to regain control and cursing in language no doubt learned from his days in the infantry. Ernie explained to me that the old horse had once been a hunter, until old age reduced it to peddling for its oats, and that, occasionally, some sound or other seemed to spook it as though it was remembering happier days, responding with sudden bursts of energy and speed.

Every fifteen minutes or so an urgent cry would go up from one of the kids on the dray. Mr Walker would be forced to pull the horse to a standstill while one of the smaller lads slipped off onto the verge. There we waited, embarrassed, while the titch unloaded his bursting bladder of steaming Tizer.

After a couple of hours we climbed a steep hill towards an impressive church steeple, travelling at a snail's pace now. Mr Walker swore encouragingly at the horse whose flanks were frothed with white. We were entering a small town, and I was glad to be anonymous among so many kids as the locals stared at us from the pavement. Eventually we passed a sign informing us that the town was Ilkeston, about ten miles from Broxtowe and over the border into Derbyshire.

"Are we in another country, Dad?" yelled Ernie's sister, Doreen, over her shoulder.

"No. It's another county," I informed her, superior.

"That's what I said, twerp," Doreen retorted tartly.

Mr Walker surprised us all by steering the horse and dray into a pub yard. He disappeared inside while we ate the last of our dried-out sandwiches and guzzled the dregs of our fizzless Tizer. After a while, Mr Walker limped out of the pub with a bucket of water. He offered it up to the horse, then ordered Ernie to wet the wheels of the dray, while he had a pint inside. Ernie took the bucket inside the pub to refill it when the weary horse had quenched its thirst. He carefully poured water over the spokes of the wheels to make them swell, and hold. Then we found a spot of shade against the pub wall and watched the Withern Road kids lark in the yard until, gradually, the heat got to them and they, too, sought out some respite from it by lying on a patch of scuffed grass that was the pub "garden", according to a sign nailed to a broken-down fence.

Mr Walker's pint seemed to be a long one. He didn't come out of the pub for what seemed like hours. He took so long over his refreshment that some of the younger kids began to complain of boredom, and the heat, begging Ernie to find them something to drink. I began to wonder if Mr Walker had forgotten we were there. When I put my doubts to Ernie, he went into the pub to find his dad. He returned with a pint of shandy, which he shared with me. "He's just having his last pint," he informed me, "and a game of dominoes." When Mr Walker did stumble out, eventually, he was in a sanguine mood, breathing beer fumes over us as he counted heads for the return journey.

Going home, the excitement had gone. The afternoon sun bore down on us as we lay lethargically on the warm floorboards of the dray, gasping for something to drink. The heat of the sun burned into my head. My lips were as dry as John Clements's when he was lost in the Sahara Desert in *Four Feathers*. I closed my eyes and thought about drinking. I was in the bar of the famous Stork Club, where all my Hollywood heroes spent their evenings. There was a tall, elegant glass in front of me, empty. I was wearing my usual white dinner jacket, and Claudette Colbert was watching me, lovingly. I beckoned Joe, the slick barman, over to me. "Give me another double Tizer on the rocks, Joe," I said in Clark Gable's voice, "and something sweet for Claudette."

Ernie was talking to his dad when I came out of my reverie on the edge of Broxtowe Estate.

"Why is it called a 'mystery trip', Dad?" He asked.

Mr Walker clucked wearily at the perspiring old horse. "Because it's a bleddy mystery why I did it," he said.

Chapter 11

Junior School

Becoming a scholar in the new Player Junior School was an unhappy experience. I had never minded going to school in the past, and had even enjoyed lessons occasionally. If I had made any progress in my education it came to an abrupt halt, now. The fault lay not so much with my attitude, or with the Luftwaffe and the sirens which kept us up late at night and made us dozy in class, but with the unfriendly ambience of the place. What I hated, and dreaded, was the rigid discipline of the teachers, and the unrelenting boredom of the lessons. Perhaps the rigid discipline was necessary of classes of 40 or more boys which was in practice self-defeating. The teaching method was uniform, and based upon learning by rote. A good memory was the key to success in most subjects, and the "fact" ruled, although I believe little in the way of understanding was possible. There was no talking in class here – not without running the risk of punishment from the ever swinging three-tongued tawse which burned red weals into the hand and made the toughest boys cry. We weren't aware that Player School was considered a "tough" school for teachers because the children originally came from slum areas in Nottingham. A few generations later, in the middle of an age of affluence, it was also designated as "deprived". In hindsight, the bad tempers of the teachers, and their bullying, might be excused as battle fatigue. But my classmates and I saw it as an overt dislike of us. The teaching was a system of communication designed to maintain the distance which lay between us and them. Answering a question correctly on some topic we drew out of the battered old text books was a passport to safety for a few minutes, and it was possible to sit back to watch your pals squirm as they waited for the dreaded finger of the teacher to point at them.

Although I got by quite comfortably in most lessons, I couldn't hide my woeful ignorance of arithmetic. I had never been adept at figures, and now a kind of blind panic set in which sent unconnected digits whirling in confusion through my brain. I wondered if I had missed some vital information about arithmetic in the past, perhaps one day when I was absent with my bad foot. How did you memorize the multiplication tables? And what was the mystery of division? I struggled to find the key to the locked door behind which lay the secrets of arithmetic. I couldn't find the key, and I was too scared of the teachers to ask for help, reluctant to reveal myself as stupid. The only comfort I had was knowing that other boys in our class were searching for that same key, and suffered along with me. Each page turned in the arithmetic text book meant more of us were lost in a fog of incomprehension. The fault lay with us, we were told, and not with the teaching method or with the teachers who treated the text as a timetable and a sacred script, not to be deviated from.

Finally, a few boys would keep up with the text book while the rest of us stumbled at various arithmetical obstacles, such as long division, in the race with the teacher. Only a neat, smartly dressed boy in a proper school blazer and polished shoes shone at arithmetic. He also wrote in perfect cursive with a fountain pen and shone at reading. Few of us spoke to him. We copied each other's mistakes and resigned ourselves to being the congenital dunces the arithmetic teacher said we were.

In other lessons we learned Gradgrind facts and copied them out. What those facts were I can't remember, but I kept up well enough, finding such work easy, if boring. But Arithmetic was king, Handwriting was queen, and as I was poor at both, my performance in other subjects didn't win me any stick-on stars in my exercise books. Fountain Pen's books, on the other hand, resembled an astronomer's star chart. A boy could win high praise for decorative handwriting. The best were sent from classroom to classroom to demonstrate good handwriting, even though the content might be worthless, a copy of some passage we couldn't understand, or didn't care about. English lessons often involved filling in missing words in a passage, or making lists of verbs, nouns or adjectives gleaned from old fashioned belles-lettres. History began with Alfred, and went on to William the Conqueror. That was my favourite lesson because it was mainly about battles, although it didn't match up to the battles I read about in the *Daily Herald*. Later we did Henry the Eighth. He had six wives, or was it eight? He bumped them off at regular intervals, but we never knew why. He looked like Charles Laughton and had piggish table manners, tossing half-eaten chickens over his shoulder at dinner. We knew this because we had seen the film at the Forum. Geography was Africa, which was black and full of ignorance by all accounts. It was populated by natives who carried spears and sometimes ate one another according to the films we saw about the continent. The women had pot bellies and pounded corn with huge pestles: the photographs in our 1920's text books showed that. Some of them were carried off by lions for supper. The luckier ones became members of the British Empire so that white men could civilize them into our ways.

There was little imaginative reading, and no poetry. Music was confined to a few hymns in morning assembly during which we shivered while the dewdrops ran as we mouthed the words of *Jerusalem*. It promised a "green and pleasant land" which I visualized as the private park around Strelley Hall. What gave this "green and pleasant land" its appeal for me was that I wouldn't be chased by a man with a dog as we sometimes were in Strelley. It would be a paradise for scrumpers. One morning I was whispering to a pal about the joys of this new Jerusalem when I felt a slap on the back of my head, followed later by a dose of the tawse. If my classmate hadn't laughed when I mentioned the scrumping opportunities waiting for us I might have got away with my lack of respect for that daft old hymn. The routine of casual violence in that place affected us in the playground and in the streets of the estate. There was much fighting in both places, and the male teachers seemed to regard this as comic. Mr Richards, my own form master, enjoyed diving in to break up a fight or swab a bloody nose. The teachers always laughed on such occasions, sharing a joke we couldn't understand. We were afraid of

Mr Richards. He was small in stature, prematurely bald and youthfully energetic – an energy which he expended on maintaining a regime of absolute discipline. There was a latent threat in his sudden, nimble movements from one side of the packed classroom to the other, often executed in a silence which brought him to your shoulder before you realized he was there. His twelve-inch ruler rapped knuckles as he stalked, quite gracefully, from desk to desk. He used the tawse for punishing unforgivable sins such as blotting an exercise book or whispering to a pal. When he made a joke, we laughed in response – not because we ever found his sarcastic humour funny, but because he was slightly less dangerous with a smile on his face. We were so afraid of him that we didn't even joke about his bald head in case it got back to him via some sneak.

It was Mr Richards who gave me my most painful dose of the tawse on the day I discovered that I could look after myself pretty well in a fist fight. Why the fight started, I can't remember, but it was sure to have been trivial. It didn't take too much provocation for a scrap to flare up between two boys. There was kudos to be won by flooring an opponent, usually the signal that the scrap was over. The contests were, paradoxically in such a graceless place, honourable affairs in which only the two protagonists could be involved. Only the fists were used, and to be so underhand as to kick your opponent was certain to result in your being ostracised for days. It was taboo, also, to take advantage of a helpless opponent by punching him when he was on the floor, especially if he was crying by that time. Why we should have been so chivalrous I don't know, but the scruffiest boy from the top-end of the estate would step back at such a point because the rest of us expected it of him. What we really fought for was the chance to frighten off other challengers, make them wary of you, win a little space for yourself. There was also the chance to win a little pride by being thought tough in a hard school.

My moment came when I was challenged by a lively, popular lad called Ivan who lived out in his play the improbable physical feats of Hollywood heroes, especially those of his favourite, the cowboy Buck Jones. He believed so much in his own invincibility that when he came at me with his fists clenched, but down by his side, I knocked him down with a straight left. There was a look of shock on his reddened face, no doubt because reality wasn't working out like the Buck Jones film running in his head. He jumped up and advanced towards me with his elbows cocked as though he was ready to draw on a pair of Colt six-shooters from imaginary holsters. He was so open as a target that I knew I was going to win my first fist fight. I was overjoyed by my rare athletic success. I hit him again, and down he slumped onto his backside, on the verge of tears. He was helped up by his tactless pals, an act which must have humiliated him further as he crept away, red faced and tearful, with an unconvincing threat that he would "get me later".

I wasn't considered a scrapper by my classmates, and I certainly didn't consider my self one, so this provoked Ivan's pals into trying to revenge his defeat. Fortunately they came at me one at a time in an orderly manner, their tactics determined by a gang of yelling spectators who gathered to watch my slaughter, as long as it was fairly executed. Necessity revealed a gift of nature I had been totally ignorant of until my moment of danger, and one which was recompense for my bad foot. I discovered I could box. I had what was known as "fast hands" in boxing parlance, and a good sense of distance which enabled me to avoid punches whilst timing my own accurately. Soon I had floored the more aggressive of Ivan's pals. The rest seemed to lose heart as they waited in the queue for their go at me, turning away like reluctant suicides. It was one of the happiest moments of my life.

Mr Richards laid on the tawse with his usual enthusiasm. But, though it was painful, and the palms of my hands were red and raw, it couldn't diminish the elation I felt at my playground triumph. Apart from discovering that I wasn't completely handicapped by my weak right foot – I was hopeless at cricket and too tentative at football – victories achieved with the fists boosted your status. There were some awkward situations later when I came close to being challenged by the scrappers with fists of granite who ruled the top-end of Broxtowe. They would have reduced me to dog-meat had I not managed to talk myself out of trouble.

My easy, unexpected defeat of Ivan – who later became a pal – didn't cure him of his insatiable, romantic delusion that he was born to be a hero. After he left school he became a telegraph boy. For three happy years he raced through the Nottingham streets on his red Post Office bike, sliding around corners in speedway style, laughing and chatting up the local office girls with his pillbox hat set at a snazzy angle on his blonde head. When he was 17 years old he joined the Royal Marines. In less than 12 months he was dead: killed in his first real battle on some god-forsaken hill in Korea.

* * *

If we were afraid of Mr Richards, he in his turn was nervous in the presence of the headmaster of Player Junior School, Mr Alkman. He was the little emperor of boys and frazzled teachers, a toby-jug replica of Winston Churchill, smaller in build, but with similar "bulldog" features. Mr Alkman played on his physical resemblance to the Prime Minister for all it was worth. Churchill was looked on by us boys as a super-human being at this time, and our awe of him influenced our feelings towards the headmaster. Like Churchill, Mr Alkman wore spectacles of the half-frame type. They sat on the end of his nose so that his eyes were always restless, his gaze flicking over or through them. His head sank into heavy shoulders which leaned forward when he walked as if the rest of his dumpy body was compelled to keep up with their forceful thrust ahead. Several times a day he patrolled the corridors, open on one side, the classrooms off the other, with his hands clasped behind his back, his bulldog head thrust aggressively forward. At each classroom door he would peer through the glass to check what the 40 boys inside the room were doing. His eyes would swivel over his spectacles, his gaze moving from the potential skivers on the back row to the teacher at the front. If a boy was talking, or rather whispering, or was slumped in an attitude of boredom, Mr Alkman would open the door to poke his head into the classroom – an act which straightened every back and encouraged a bout of hectic scribbling. "Any problems, Mr Richards? Mrs Daft?" The question might have been directed as an oblique reprimand to a teacher if he, or she, was daydreaming about their pension at the desk, or gazing out of the window. Mr Richards nearly jumped out of his skin sometimes when the classroom door was yanked open, even if it was only a boy with a message. Following a visit by Mr Alkman, Mr Richards would spark into action, springing to his feet and slapping his palm with his ruler as a warning we all understood.

In morning assembly Mr Alkman's ego blossomed. He was an actor whose calculated delivery was aimed at achieving the maximum dramatic effect, although it was torture for us. His favourite text when he preached to us was Being A Good Citizen. The challenge of transforming 400 unenthusiastic, unacademic, ragamuffin barbarians into Good Citizens seemed to be his prime motivation, the holy grail of education itself. Actually, I quite liked the sound of the word "citizen", in spite of not knowing what it meant. So grand did it sound that I imagined you had to be pretty posh to become one.

One morning we marched in twos into the hall, arranged ourselves in straight rows across the parquet floor, then sat down on it, shoulder to shoulder, our legs crossed uniformly. The morning whispers between the boys were stilled at Mr Alkman's theatrical entry. He strode onto the stage, peering over his spectacles at us, then stood in silence to build up the tension. We froze into absolute silence on the cold parquet floor, transfixed, almost. Then he addressed us: "Some of you are team players; some of you are not. Some of you learn your lessons; some of you are too idle. But what you can all be if you make the effort is a Good Citizen. And what is a Good Citizen? Put your arm down, boy! A Good Citizen is one who serves his country, and we can all serve our country in some way. Hands up anyone who has a member of their family in the armed services!"

There was a flutter of uncertainty. Did he mean in the army or the navy? A few timid arms were slowly raised into the air. Mr Alkman was irritated by the lack of drama in response to his inquiry. "Who's got a dad or a brother or an uncle in the army, the navy or the airforce?" he demanded tetchily.

Nearly every boy in the hall thrust an arm into the air. I thought for a moment that as the children of servicemen we were about to receive a free gift. We had been presented with Horlicks tablets once.

"Well, if your relative is in the services it means he is doing his duty. Hands down. And that is what being a Good Citizen means: doing your duty for your king and country. But you are too young to do your duty in the services, so you have to be Good Citizens in other ways. In what other ways do you think you can be Good Citizens?"

There was no response to this, and Mr Alkman thrust his big jaw forward – a sure sign that he was losing patience with us. He paced the stage, waiting for an arm to shoot up, and we waited for the volcano to erupt. "What's wrong with you all this morning? Are you still asleep. Haven't you woken up yet. Are you all stupid?"

None of us really understood what answer was required. Even Fountain Pen looked puzzled. We fidgeted before one of the top-end scruffs surprised us all by lifting his arm.

"Yes?" Mr Alkman demanded, pointing.

"Help your mam with the errands," the scruff suggested.

We laughed, relieved, expecting our ridicule to be supported by a contemptuous snort from Mr Alkman. But he surprised us.

"That's right!" he barked, loud enough to quell the laughter. "Helping your mother with the errands. Helping with the washing up. Doing what you are told. Being polite. Obeying the rules. But there are many other ways you can make a start on the road to becoming a Good Citizen. In fact, I can tell you now which of you have made that start. How do you think I know that? How can I tell which of you will become a Good Citizen one day?"

This was too deep for us. He had lost us, and not a single arm went up.

"Well, I will tell you. A Good Citizen of the future will always take care of his appearance. He will be clean. Good Citizens wash before they come to school. They wash their faces and they wash behind their ears. They wear a clean shirt, and keep their socks pulled up. I can tell straight away if a boy is going to be a Good Citizen. Do you know what I look at first?"

Fountain Pen must have felt duty bound as a potential Good Citizen to put his arm up.

"Yes?" Mr Alkman snapped.

"Clean ears, sir."

"Clean ears are important, certainly. But that's not the first thing I look for." He paused as if he was about to reveal the secret of the universe. "I look at his boots. If a boy has polished his boots or his shoes I know he is on the way to becoming a Good Citizen."

He peered over the top of his spectacles. "How many of you have polished their boots or shoes this morning?"

A dozen Good Citizens put their arms up. I wasn't one of them.

"Not many is it? It's disgraceful, disgraceful. Well, I'm going to walk through you, and I want you to take a good look at my shoes."

He clasped his hands behind his back and descended the short flight of steps from the stage to the floor of the hall. He faced the congregation, moving towards us with a casual deliberation that showed how much of an actor he was. He would probably have walked over the first row of seated boys if they hadn't shuffled on their bottoms to let him pass – Moses parting the sea. No word of command was necessary: we all shuffled sideways to clear a passage for him. His progress was stately as boys focused on his gleaming brogues. He glanced from face to face as though he was searching for a particular boy. Stopping at last he jabbed a stumpy finger at a startled top-end scruff. "You! Have I polished my shoes this morning?"

The scruff was staring into Mr Alkman's face like a mesmerized rabbit. "Yes sir."

"Look at my shoes, not at me!"

The scruff lowered his gaze. "Yes sir."

Mr Alkman grunted and strolled on. As he approached the rear of the hall, where I was trying to melt into the parquet, I could hear the faint, healthy creak of polished leather emanating from every precisely trodden step. I could see the brogues clearly now. They were immaculate, glass-like toe-caps gleaming. There was no doubt that he was an Exemplary Citizen. He reached my row, and I knew that I would be his victim. I couldn't remember when I had last polished my shoes, and the skin had been scraped off them long ago. Mr Alkman's mocking blue eyes sought mine out. I tried not look at him, tucking my shoes under my legs. I wondered if the hole in the heel of my sock had worked up from under my foot where I had tucked it. I daren't look – I was doomed anyway.

"Your shoes are a disgrace! When did you last polish them? At christmas?"

There was relieved laughter from the tense congregation. The bad example had been selected: I was not destined to be a Good Citizen.

"What's your name, young man?"

"Buttress sir." My face burned as it always did when I had to speak my name out loud. It sounded so odd, and sometimes people laughed.

"Buttress," Mr Alkman repeated. "Well, I wouldn't like you to support me!" There was another cackle of laughter from the congregation, although I was sure that only Fountain Pen and I understood his joke.

How I despised him – not only for ridiculing my name, but for the arrogance of his strutting walk through us, and for the assumption that I wouldn't understand his attempt at wit, know what a buttress was. He had smiled slyly across at Mr Richards who stood with his arms folded at the side of the hall. My teacher returned the invitation to share the joke with the smile of a sycophant.

That night I rubbed dollops of Cherry Blossom polish into my ruined shoes in an effort to redeem the neglect, disguise the abuse my play had scraped into them. I didn't want to be a Good Citizen, anyway, if it made you turn into a Mr Alkman or a Mr Richards. What I did want was to avoid being picked out and exposed again. The incident cut deep: but it taught me anonymity was the surest way to avoid trouble from those who wanted to shape me in their own image. I arrived at that knowledge more by instinct than by thinking it through. I didn't want to be like Dad, or any of my teachers. In spite of having little idea of who or what I was, I just wanted to be left alone, to be me, imagining that one day I would grow up to be a hero of some kind, perhaps one to match the heroes of Hollywood.

As much as I disliked it, school could not be avoided. To escape, occasionally, I managed to persuade Mam that my foot was giving me trouble, and sometimes it was. On pain-free days I made a miraculous recovery before midday, so she must have known I was skiving, but didn't seem to mind because I was available for errands and pot washing. It didn't occur to me that being absent with such regularity would make me more conspicuous, not less. I made matters worse by truanting now and again. Mam's sister, Aunt Edie, connived in this deceit when I walked into her house on my way to school. I ran errands for her, or kept my eye on my toddler cousin, June, while she toddled off for a gossip and a cup of tea with her cronies leaving me to listen to *Music While You Work* on the radio, blissfully ignorant of the irony.

It wasn't long before the School Attendance Officer – the "schoolboard man" – came looking for me. He was a swarthy-looking character whose thick-lensed glasses magnified his eyes alarmingly. If I spotted him at the shops, which he hung around hoping to catch school-shy miscreants, I usually darted into the gloomy Co-op and positioned myself behind the largest woman available. He never actually came into a shop, so this ploy worked. Sometimes, though, he would appear as if from nowhere when I was strolling up or down Bradfield Road, and exposed. Thus I was trapped, my stuttered excuse for not being at school sounding ridiculously feeble when he grilled me. One day he caught me totally by surprise as I dribbled a tin-can down the hill on my way to the shops. His eyes grew big in triumph through those sinister glasses. He opened his note book, scribbled something in it.

"Why aren't you in school?" he demanded fiercely.

"I've got a bad foot, sir," I mumbled.

"You're Buttress, aren't you?"

"Yes sir."

"Your bad foot doesn't stop you playing football, does it? I've dealt with you before, haven't I?"

"Yes sir."

"Does your mother know you're not at school?"

"She made me stay at home," I lied, "because of my bad foot."

"You look all right to me." He wrote something in his notebook. "Does your mother know she can be prosecuted for not sending you to school?"

"I don't know, sir." Mam probably did know, but it wouldn't bother her too much. She regularly received threats of prosecution from firms she owed money to.

"I don't know." He sighed, a dismissive exhalation of exasperation that the insignificant such as I should cause him so much trouble. He scribbled furiously in his notebook, then seemed to lose his temper.

"You'll never learn, Buttress. You'll never learn. Your sort are a waste of time."

With that he brushed past me, striding up Bradfield Road to leave his words like a knife in my chest. Tears stung my eyes, but I fought them back. *It's not true. It's not true. I'm not a waste of time!* I told myself as I ran to the shops.

A few days later a letter of warning arrived from the Education Department, a threat that if my attendance at school didn't improve drastically my parents would be prosecuted. The threat wasn't needed. I was horrified that the schoolboard man knew my name, wrote about me in his notebook, and that the Education Department were monitoring my skiving and my truancy. Whether or not they were monitoring the sterility of the teaching at the John Player Junior School at that time, I don't know. But I was ready for entry into the senior school by then, and that opened up a far different future for me than the one predicted by the schoolboard man.

Grandfather and Grandmother. Harry Anderson Buttress (1882–1954) and
Ada Buttress (1883–1966) during the First World War.

My sister, Brenda, and myself in 1936. Taken in the backyard of the house in Portland Road. The Arboretum was close by, and became a favourite playground.

My mother and her sisters, with a friend. 'Mam' (Ada) is in the centre of the group. Her sister, Mabel, is immediately in front of her. Edie is next to Mabel, and Ida is at the other end with a cardigan over her arm. A friend stands between Ada and Ida.

63, Hollis Street, New Basford, is marked with a cross. I was born there on January 2nd, 1932. The Buttress family lived there from 1914 to 1966.

Adolf Hitler peels an apple. This image would have provoked uncouth laughter from the regulars in the Forum Cinema if they had seen it on the screen.

We were more used to seeing Hitler as a uniformed Nazi. But even this shot of him signing his autograph for a member of the Hitler Youth shows him in too 'human' a pose for the British newsreels.

The new, and very clean Nottingham Council House in 1930.

Plumtre Place, Lace Market. This backstreet led to the rear entrance of
Priestly and Swann, printers and box-makers. Note the metal hitching posts.
Beneath the road lay cellars housing large lithographic printing machines
producing labels for many of the lace and hosiery factories in the area.

Stoney Street, the Lace Market's main thoroughfare. Little has changed externally in the last hundred years, although a number of the warehouses have been transormed into 'luxury' apartments.

A typical example of wartime propaganda. No doubt this postcard was designed for an optimistic wife to send to her husband in the forces.

Strelley village and church. A favourite destination for Broxtowe folk out for a walk.

The Beacon, Aspley Lane. Although this is a recent photograph, the exterior of the pub has hardly changed since 1940.

The senior school hall, John Player School, Denewood Crescent, Bilborough as it is today. The campus now houses a Social Services Centre.

Withern Road, Broxtowe Estate as it is today. Hedges and shrubs have softened the raw appearance it presented in the 1940's.

All Saints, Strelley, It contains a fine alabaster tomb-chest with effigies of Sir Sampson de Strelley and his wife which dates from c. 1400, as well as other medieval works of art.

Chapter 12

Bookworm

School was boring, but there was no escape from it. My brush with the schoolboard man had taught me that. I had an appetite for reading which was unsatisfied by the starvation rations offered by the Junior School's tired text books and the fragments of imaginative literature used by our teachers for purposes other than feeding the imagination. At home, reading was considered a way of passing the time, adding a bit of interest to doing nothing. Usually it was considered an activity for the idle, an excuse for skiving. There were one or two books in the house, occasionally: pulp thrillers that Cousin Arthur had given me. Even Mam and Aunt Mabel read, sometimes, but only the weekly romance papers which they called "books". *Lucky Star* and *Red Letter* were their favourites, and I read them too, simply because there was nothing else. They featured short stories with titles such as *Bad Girl* and *He Did Her Wrong*, usually about an honest working-class girl who was made pregnant by some swine with a sports car and bags of money. Men were either shallow lotharios, or honest but lumpen working lads, who always made the best husbands. There was often a drawing of the wronged heroine walking down the terraced street with her head down in shame while older women whispered about her with sneering disapproval of her "sin" as they stood, their arms folded, on their doorsteps. I read such stories, although they provided little that engaged the imagination, and were not as interesting as the "true" stories in the *Daily Herald* and the *Evening Post*.

Relief for my word starvation arrived casually, accidentally, the consequences of which were to alter the course of my life, although I could understand that only in hindsight many years later. I was on a bus travelling to Aspley, our neighbouring council estate, on some errand when Fountain Pen slumped into the seat beside me. He was carrying two hard-backed books with red leatherette covers. He told me he was on his way to Aspley Public Library to change them.

"How much does it cost?" I asked.

"Nothing. You can borrow them for free. I change them every Saturday. My mam doesn't let me go out much, so I read a lot."

That was no surprise. He was, after all, the brainiest lad in the school.

"How do you get in the library?" I asked, wondering if you had to pass an intelligence test.

"Anybody can join. It's easy," he informed me. "You just go in and tell the woman at the desk that you want to join."

Returning from my errand I dropped off the bus at the library, hung outside the glass doors for a few minutes, peeping inside whenever anybody went in, trying to pluck up the nerve to enter and speak to the posh-looking woman at the desk. Eventually I crept in and asked the woman if I could join.

"You'll have to take this card home for your mother to sign. When you bring it back you can borrow two books, but you must bring them back within two weeks. You can have a look round first," she added, and smiled. "The Junior Library is through that door."

I entered the room and felt like yelling in joy. I had never seen so many books in one place, and all for children. Even the smell was beguiling. It would take me for ever to read them all, and the prospect was wonderful. The room was brightly lit and furnished with round tables the colour of honey. Around them there were child-sized chairs with upholstered seats – sheer luxury! Against a wall stood a peculiar wooden projection which looked like the skeleton of an enormous fan. From it hung copies of *The Children's Newspaper*, but they seemed dull reading. A low cabinet was packed with encyclopaedias, one of which I examined. It seemed to contain everything there was to know in the world, but that wasn't what I wanted to read, so I jammed it back in its row. High shelving against the walls was divided into sections: History, Hobbies and Games, Nature, Other Lands and Science. But covering at least half of the walls was Fiction – case after case of it from the floor to the high windows. This was exactly what I was looking for.

When I returned about an hour later with my card signed by Mam, I made straight for the fiction shelves. There was so much of it, and so tantalising was the choice, that I didn't know where to look first. A boy wearing the flash blazer and badge of the High Pavement Grammar School strolled in while I gazed up in bewilderment at the walls of fiction. He sauntered around the library with a casual ease that I envied.

"Hiya!" he said cheerily. "Found anything good?"

"I'm just looking," I mumbled, feeling like a trespasser.

"You brought any William books back?"

"No," I said, thinking he at least shared my interest in William the Conqueror – probably a requirement for a grammar school boy.

"Do you like William books?" he asked.

"They're okay. We've done him at our school. I like stories, though."

"William books are stories," he said, not put out by my ignorance. "About this mad boy called William. They're really wizard."

He strolled across to the "C" section of the shelves, searched for a moment, pulled out a book and brought it over to me. "Try this," he said.

I read the title on the spine: *William the Rebel*. The author was a bloke called Richmal Crompton.

"You read it," he said with evangelical enthusiasm. "It's really, really funny!"

I began to read it at the bus stop. Then I read it on the bus. I read it as I walked down Frinton Road, and carried on reading when I reached home. Now I was in a world populated by comic boys fighting a never-ending battle with potty adults and getting into the kind of scrapes that would have earned me a clout from Mam, but which William Brown got away with. His worst punishment was to spend an early night in the awesome luxury of a room to himself. The plotted daftness made me giggle to myself, Aunt Mabel giving me funny looks, probably suspicious that I might be cheekily sniggering at her. I persevered in my reading through the gossip of Mam and

Aunt Mabel, through their complaints that I was under their feet, and through the chirpy play of Peter and Michael who climbed all over me to divert my attention from the book. But they couldn't. I went to bed that night thankful that, through Fountain Pen and the grammar school boy, my word starvation was behind me. I read until Mam switched the light off in the bedroom because I was wasting the penny in the meter. The Aspley Public Library was the door through which I could escape, allowing nothing and no-one to touch me – neither Mam, Aunt Mabel, Dad, Mr Alkman and Mr Richards, nor the schoolboard man.

There were other discoveries to be made in this unexpected treasure of free reading matter. One surprising fact was that Richmal Crompton was a woman. How could a woman know so much about kids like William? She was certainly smarter than Mam and Mabel, and a million times smarter than teachers like Mrs Daft at school. But the world William lived in was a lot different to mine. Maids opened doors, Cooks made lunch, which was really dinner, parents had dinner parties and soirees, whatever they were, wearing bow ties and long frocks. School wasn't mentioned much, and then only when William was in trouble there. William and his gang even had their own hut for meetings, and the sun was usually shining on their carefree world. I was drawn to William's world because of its difference from mine, just as I was drawn to William because he was relentlessly inventive, bold, and resisted all attempts to civilize him. I was drawn, too, into the world of public-school stories because they played out in their own elite way the battle between adult rule and the anarchic free spirit of boys. I ignored the snobbery as the norm in stories – stories were written by the posh, so why worry that they were set in a posh world and spoke in a posh accent, unless the character was a handyman or gardener – then he spoke common because he wasn't very bright. I enjoyed the fun, even though I would never be able to open my mouth to speak in my common accent if I met somebody from that world of *Topping Towers*.

In contrast I read strange, disturbing stories by the Grimm Brothers, tales which I visualised as movies from the Disney studio, and in the style of the scene in *Snow White* when the beautiful but evil Queen transforms herself into an ugly witch. I wrapped the covers of the library book in brown paper to conceal the evidence from my pals that I was reading "fairy stories". I read whatever took my fancy with no direction or interference. I read to suit my mood, and that could lead me to a Biggles adventure, which I thought were rather boring, or to the potted biographies of imperialist heroes such as Wolfe of Quebec and Clive of India. I read and re-read, lovingly, Kipling's *Jungle Book* and *Just So Stories* then skimmed with faint contempt through cruder stories set in the British Empire which related the doing and daring of stiffly moral Englishmen in battle against blacks, Indians and Polynesians. These English gentlemen soldiers and adventurers fought against the odds with guns and cutlasses because the revolting natives were too ignorant to accept civilization when they had the chance. The quality of the writing mattered to me, although I couldn't have explained why. Some novels were hard to read because they were written in a complicated syntax which was as challenging to a juvenile reader as a cliff face is to a novice climber. Sometimes I gave up if the language and syntax was beyond me. As I gained in experience I discovered that difficulty can provide its own reward. There was a sense of achievement waiting if I got to the end of a challenging book, even if I had not entirely mastered it. Once at the end of a read that had demanded all my concentration I felt that I had made the book my own. In this way I struggled through Dicken's *Tale of Two Cities*, *A Christmas Carol* and *Oliver Twist* as well as Jack London's *White Fang* and Stevenson's *Treasure Island* like a climber who risks his neck knowing that his effort will reward him with a glimpse of the landscape on top of the cliff, a country of the mind and imagination that only he, of all the people he knows, will be aware of.

Mr Alkman and Mr Richards would have approved of this serious reading had they known about it, although I don't remember ever being encouraged to read in their school, except by Fountain Pen, and outside of school by Cousin Arthur. Perhaps Mr Alkman might have thought my choice of reading matter too eclectic as well as too insular an activity. Was reading alone, especially about the comic activities of William Brown, conducive to learning how to be a Good Citizen? Mr Richards might well have asked me if such verbal gluttony improved my poor retention of the multiplication tables which I sing-songed every morning on their passage through my numbed brain and into oblivion.

The only immediate measurable effect my visits to the library had on my school career was to make me top of the class in the regular reading tests. It was a phenomenon which seemed to surprise Mrs Daft, who carried them out, and upset the long established order of merit, placing me above a resentful Fountain Pen. He was unaware that he was partially responsible for his own downfall, the innocent instigator of my first tentative moves towards a haphazard self-education.

Chapter 13

Ernie, Mo and Me

The constant rows between Mam and Dad was my secret, one I carried with me as a dull weight of shame, a handicap I thought best to hide from my friends like an embarrassed cripple. I considered it grossly unfair to have been selected to live in a home with such warring parents. I was sure a mistake must have been made. Apart from hating their rows, I had been allocated parents who didn't recognize my finer points, and who were blind to the possibility of happiness. I heard laughter in my friends' homes and resented its being so severely rationed in my own. Such thoughts only exacerbated my frequent bouts of tearful self-pity.

I felt, at times, that I was living parallel lives: one set in the battlefield of home, the other one a completely different existence in the careless, self-sufficient world of the Broxtowe streets. Lost in play, immersed in the plots and fancies of the kids on Withern Road, two streets away and out of sight of home, I became someone that Mam and Dad might not have recognized. Here the world was simple: its puzzles and uncertainties were pushed aside behind thoughtless banter and jokes, catch phrases culled from the wireless, arguments that were forgotten in an hour, our personalities as easy to read as those of characters in the *Rover* or the *Hotspur* story papers. The images of home – the four plain chairs around the table, the sideboard with its junk-stuffed drawers, the black painted fireplace, the hand-pegged rag mat in front of it – all lurked in my mind as irritating symbols of Mam and Dad's fraught relationship, the unhappy life of which I was a part, one which I must return to but which I could turn my back on for a few hours in the company of my pals Ernie and Mo, Yank, Marion and Jean.

Although Ernie and Mo were my closest friends, we rarely talked about our parents, or about what went off inside our homes. Neither did we give much time to the past, or to anticipating the future except to think that the latter couldn't begin until we won the war. The years beyond that point were a void except for hazy images of ourselves as adults – strong, tough, looked up to, leaders – so different to our parents that they wouldn't recognize us as their own ragamuffin offspring. But such moments of speculation were rare. The important time was *now*; this minute, this second. The rest of time belonged to our parents, and they were welcome to it.

* * *

Ernie fancied himself as an entrepreneur, just like his dad, hoping one day that he would inherit the old man's horse and dray, along with his firewood round. One of his first ventures was to buy a load of bundled firewood himself, hire a handcart, then go touting for customers on the Aspley estate. Anyone who went to call for him to come out to play was recruited as a salesman to assist in the enterprise. I was the world's worst salesman. I was too self-conscious to open my mouth, stuttering incomprehensibly when a front door was opened and an impatient householder glared at me. The pathetically few bundles I sold were probably bought out of pity rather than a desire to light a fire.

Mo, a lad who lived a few doors from Ernie, was also recruited to the salesforce. He was even worse at it than I was. He suffered the handicap of weak eyes, one of which had a twitchy cast. You never knew whether or not he was looking at you when he spoke or at some point over your shoulder. When a door opened to him, he would stare at the doorstep, mumbling with his head down. In the company of Ernie and me, he was more relaxed, laughing with us, but always self-conscious about his poor eyes and the fact that he attended a school for less able pupils, which the cruellest of kids called "the daft school". Barrel-chested, with heavy shoulders and huge fists, he had fights with lads passing down the street who were foolish enough to mock his squint. They always ended up being escorted home in a dazed condition by their pals. When Mo hit an adversary it was Good-Night Vienna, no matter how big his opponent was. He took a lot of pride in his right uppercut, a punch he swung from the floor although there was no guarantee that he would hit what he was aiming for.

Mercifully, I was spared first-hand knowledge of his uppercut as we got on well together, but I had to be on my guard against making sarcastic comments in response to his almost total ignorance of the world. He considered me something of a scholar, a pal who was useful to have around when any reading was called for, such as signs declaring "Trespassers Will Be Prosecuted".

Just how poor he was academically became apparent to me when I found him down his air-raid shelter one day painfully studying two versions of a love letter he had laboriously composed. They were written to a pretty girl called Marion who had recently moved into Withern Road. She had wide, fawn-like eyes and a soft black fringe. I rather fancied her myself. At first I thought they were intended for a girl called Marjorie because they were addressed to "margarine", and that would have been close for Mo.

The first one read: "der margarine i lov yu lov mo".

"It should read 'Marjorie'," I said.

"I don't know no Marjorie," Mo said. "It's for Marion."

"She won't like being called 'Margarine'."

"It's not 'Margarine'," Mo said. "It's Marge. I copied it off a Stork wrapper. Marge is short for 'Marion'."

"No it isn't!" I protested.

"It'll do!" Mo snapped. He was getting impatient. As far as he was concerned all this fuss over spelling was irrelevant. "Which one's best?" he asked, handing me another scrap of paper torn out of an exercise book.

The second version was more passionate: "der margarine i lov yu very much lov mo".

"This one's best". How could Marion resist such a declaration?

Mo tore the first version in half. He sent the second version to Marion via her young brother, but received no reply. A few days later Marion became the first girl I kissed because I wanted to, while Mo looked on, biting on his thumb nail.

By now I had learned that one way to keep a friend was to tell them anything they wanted to hear. Friendship was more important to me than hurtful truth. I lied to Mo because it was a small price to pay for his company. What he sought from me, constantly, was the assurance that he was tall. He was obsessed by the dream of becoming tall at some point in the near future. For him, tallness would be a confirmation of manhood, a condition he could aspire to and which would change his relationship with a world he could barely see. He hoped that a few more inches of bone and brawn would make him someone to fear a little, overcome the handicap of his rotten eyesight. Actually, he was of average height for his age, the same as Ernie and me, although he was broader and stronger than either of us. I managed to convince him that he was a head taller than us, and that he would eventually be tall enough to join the Grenadier Guards, which was his abiding dream.

"D'you reckon I'm tall?" he would ask, stretching his spine and trying to peer over the top of my head.

"Yeah, you're pretty tall," I always answered, trying to shrink an inch.

"How tall?"

"Very tall."

"Six foot?"

It was the magical measurement he longed for.

"Not quite. You will be, though."

"D'you reckon our dad's tall?" he persisted.

"Yeah, he's *very* tall."

His dad was about five feet eight inches, a thin streak of misery who always moaned about Mo's "trouser arse hangin' out" when he passed us in the street.

"How tall is he?" Mo asked.

"About six foot," I lied.

"D'you reckon I'll be tall enough for the Grenadier Guards when I'm eighteen?"

"It's a dead cert," I said, but wondered if they took half blind, boz-eyed conscripts.

As a reward for my confidence-boosting fibs Mo allowed me into his house on a Saturday night after his parents had gone on their weekly jaunt to the Cocked Hat. I always looked forward to Mo's invitation because there was a gramophone in the house. We played his sister's worn out records over and over again, the Ink Spots, Bing Crosby and the Ambrose Orchestra, mainly. There was no music in our house, not even a wireless for much of the time. This made Mo's machine even more desirable. Popular music was something I was beginning to love, a luxury I enjoyed at Ernie's house or at one of my aunt's. My favourite kind of music came from the big bands, even though it was only the tinny, watered-down sound of bands broadcasting from London's West End nightclubs. One blacked-out night I heard the sound of band music from a house on Withern Road. I crept up to the window, knelt down in a clump of heady-scented marigolds and listened to the Roy Fox band tootling its way through a swing arrangement. I was hooked for life. I still had the excitement of Benny Goodman, Tommy Dorsey and the great Arty Shaw band waiting for me in the future. But that night I was thrilled by Fox's easy-on-the-ear arrangements of the latest tunes. Like books, music offered an alternative reality, a dream world perhaps, but a necessary one.

Ernie's favourite music was the sound of cash jingling in his pocket. Eventually, he got bored with pushing the loaded handcart and when the schoolboard man threatened because he was missing school, Ernie gave up his business. His money-making became more casual as well as more dishonest. He collected rags and junk, some of it nicked from people's clothes lines, sheds and air-raid shelters, selling it to a scrapyard. He dug up potatoes, cut off cabbages and cauliflowers from Dig For Victory allotments to sell from door to door. I accompanied him on one of these selling sprees. I was recognized by somebody who knew Mam as I carried a cabbage for Ernie, and the next day suffered the ignominy of a visit from a special constable. Fortunately he didn't take the crime any further after Mam promised to give me a "bloody good hiding" as punishment. I got away without the beating because she wouldn't hit me to suit an outsider, especially one dressed in a policeman's uniform who she knew as a labourer at the Raleigh cycle factory, and a bit of an idiot to boot. Her clouts, swipes and slaps were reserved for the occasions when I broke *her* rules. I had also promised never to break the law again. She knew I meant it because the special's visit had scared me to death.

Mo and I became involved in one of Ernie's more imaginative escapades. On one of our explorations of the parkland around Strelley Hall we had discovered a plantation dangerously close to the big house. Too nervous to enter it on our first visit – we had never been so close to the house before – we returned one afternoon when we felt more daring. Like other small woods in that undulating, pretty but prohibited landscape it was dark, dense with undergrowth, and alive with mysterious scuffles and squarks. Ernie scared us by reporting that he had seen gigantic alsatians patrolling the park when he was on one of his lone forays. He could have been romancing, but nevertheless I kept glancing over my shoulder half-expecting to see the Hound of the Baskervilles bursting out of a copse.

The sounds we heard were probably made by blackbirds which followed our erratic progress through their overgrown domain making alarmed flutterings and warning calls. There were rhododendron shrubs in the plantation, glowing in full colour. Hundreds of blooms shone in a darkness which couldn't dim the beautiful mauves, pinks and violets. We yanked off handfuls of blooms to throw at each other like richly coloured snowballs. It was a secret place, and it was ours by right of discovery. Crab-apple trees grew close to the iron fence enclosing the plantation. These bore fruit which we knew would be sweet when it was ripe. That, too, would be ours when the scrumping season started. Ernie, Mo and I revelled in the place. It was like a primeval garden, long abandoned, but brought back to life by our presence.

Ernie had stopped throwing the blooms. He was examining one of them.

"What's the matter?" I asked. "What're you looking at?"

"Stop spoiling 'em," Ernie said, lost in thought.

"Nobody ever sees 'em anyway. What does it matter?"

"We're wasting 'em. They're too nice to spoil. Leave 'em alone."

His aesthetic valuation surprised me. Usually Ernie's assessment of the world around him was based on its monetary value. I should have known better than to believe, as I did for a moment, that he had suddenly developed good taste.

"I'm going home for my tea," he said, turning his back on us. "Are you coming?"

Of course we were coming. Mo and I did everything that Ernie asked of us.

He crashed through the undergrowth. Mo and I following like lambs down the path our leader had made. I could tell that his brain was already ticking over with a plan. But he wouldn't tell Mo and me until he was ready. "Come for me after tea!" he yelled as I left them at the end of Withern Road.

When I returned about an hour later I went straight to Ernie's house. He handed me a rolled-up sack. "What's this for?" I asked. It smelled sweetly of hay. Ernie had one himself, and Mo had his tucked under his arm as he leaned on the dustbin, looking somewhat puzzled, but asking no questions.

"I want some of them flowers," Ernie said. "As many as we can get."

"What're you going to do with a load of flowers?" I knew it wouldn't be because of a sudden interest in botany.

He wouldn't tell us what his plan was. I knew that it would involve making money. An Ernie plan usually meant two things: he would keep all the profits; I would get into trouble.

In fading light the plantation was more eerie than it had been in the afternoon, the scuffles in the undergrowth more sinister. The Hound of the Baskervilles loomed large in my imagination. Mo and I snapped off the rhododendron blooms to a length Ernie had indicated, while he cut his with his mam's scissors. We soon had the sacks full as he had ordered us not to cram in the blooms too tightly in case they got crushed. I was glad to scramble out of the plantation and into the open. We trotted across the park, scattering startled rabbits hopping about outside their sandy warren.

"What're you going to do with 'em?" I asked for the fiftieth time, and out of breath.

But Ernie enjoyed teasing Mo and me. "You'll see," was all he offered, enigmatically and with a sly smile on his face. We dumped the sacks outside his back door with instructions not to call for him until the following afternoon, which is what we usually did on Sunday afternoons anyway.

Sunday afternoons were always dull in spirit. The tradition of silent Sundays still persisted: the whole world was locked away for the day, and children were expected to keep quiet. Religious observance had little to do with it, directly. The tradition our parents had inherited was the chance of a rest in the sullen limbo after a week's work, a period of recuperation before the Monday millstone rolled round again. As I slouched down to Ernie's house a leaden sky was in league with the slumbering day to depress the end of the weekend. I was pondering on how I could get into the Forum, somehow, without a halfpenny in my pocket. The problem at least kept the thought of Monday, and school, at bay. I had been caught too many times trying to sneak in without paying to try that. The cinema doors opened at five o'clock on Sundays for a single performance. It meant an early closing to the weekend as the show finished about eight o'clock. If the Hollywood worshippers, like me, missed it then Sunday sank into miserable oblivion. There was nothing worse than having to mooch outside the Forum, stony broke, while all your pals were warmly cocooned in their ninepenny seats, laughing their heads off at Abbott and Costello or The Three Stooges. This anxiety about the last hours of the weekend petering out into nothingness had made me forget all about the rhododendrons.

"You're late," Ernie reprimanded when I pushed open his back gate. Mo was already there, looking rather disgruntled about something. Ernie disappeared into the house, and came out again with a cardboard box full of rhododendron blooms. Each slightly wilted flower had been tarted up with a piece of silver foil so that it looked like an extravagant, oversized buttonhole of the sort that people wore in their lapels at a wedding. The cardboard box had been turned into a tray by the simple method of looping string through holes stabbed in the sides.

"What's that?" I demanded, knowing full well that I was about to become a salesman again.

"They're buttonholes for the British Legion," Ernie explained. "We sell 'em for sixpence each, and the money goes to wounded soldiers." He hung the box around my neck, the string cutting into the flesh. "You do one side of Withern Road. Mo'll do the other."

He darted into the house again. I felt ridiculous – like the woman who sold the ice-cream at the Forum. I glanced across at Mo. He was absorbed in biting his pared down thumb nail, a sure sign that he wasn't happy. Ernie came out with a second box, which he hung on Mo.

"Right," Ernie said, businesslike. "You knock on the door, then you show 'em your licence."

"What licence?" I asked.

"Oh yeah," Ernie said, remembering. He pulled out two dog-eared postcards from his trouser pocket. "Show 'em this, then say: please buy a buttonhole to help the wounded soldiers." He handed me the postcard. I had to repeat the spiel until I was fluent enough to satisfy Ernie. He thought better of testing Mo. One glance at Mo's face perhaps convinced him that asking for such a feat of remembering might not be diplomatic. Ernie took out a flipped dog-end as though he was going to enjoy a quiet smoke in the back garden while Mo and I flogged his stolen flowers.

"Where's your box?" I demanded, aggrieved.

"I've still got some more to make," he explained, and lit up, glancing over his shoulder to make sure his mam or dad weren't in the kitchen.

His casual lie annoyed me. "You aren't giving no money to the British Legion!" I argued. "Or to wounded soldiers! You're going to keep it all yourself." I was no fool.

Ernie looked hurt, but he was a born liar. "No I'm not! You ask our old man. He's gunna tek it down the Legion hisself!"

Another lie, I had no doubt. But even when we knew he was deceiving us we went along with him. Neither Mo nor I would seriously challenge Ernie's right to make us do things. We might protest, but we wouldn't turn our backs on him. He led, because his personality gave him that right. It was a law of nature that the meek, and the backward, should obey the quick-witted, the cunning and the adventurous. I examined my licence. Scrawled in pencil was "British Legion Club. Nottingham Branch". It was obviously copied, because it was spelled correctly.

Mo and I walked up Withern Road together. "I feel right stupid," Mo said.

"He's a rob-dog," I protested. "He's going to take money off wounded soldiers."

"I feel a right prat," Mo reiterated, staring gloomily into his box of buttonholes.

Timidly, I knocked on the door of the first house on the road. A woman opened up, plainly annoyed by the interruption to her Sunday. A Victor Sylvester fox-trot danced out of the living room. "Yes?" she demanded.

My mind went blank. The words of Ernie's spiel scattered in panic.

"What do you want?" She picked up one of the buttonholes. "What's this?"

"They're flowers," I stuttered.

"I can see they're flowers! What're they for?"

"Do you want one?" I enquired hopefully.

"How much are they?"

"Sixpence." They seemed too expensive, suddenly.

"I'll give you twopence for one," she offered. She was half-smiling now as if at some memory.

I was relieved to have made a sale at my first attempt. It was only when I closed the gate behind me that I remembered I hadn't shown the woman my licence. I met with stubborn sales resistance at the first few houses I tried. But in spite of my lack of success I grew in confidence, ignoring the grubby postcard-cum-licence and offered my own fumbling spiel. The more desperate I got, the more success I had. Perhaps I looked rather pathetic with that stupid box hanging around my neck. I spoke in what was almost a whisper, just like characters do in movies when they're on their last legs. I spoke like that because I was embarrassed, as well as shy, but it was dramatically effective. Eventually a woman paid the full sixpence, although at the house next door a miserable old man in a greasy waistcoat threatened to set his hysterical Jack Russell on me as he held it up by its collar, almost strangling it, its stumpy legs frantically kicking air.

At the last house on the road a young soldier opened the front door. He laughed when he saw me on the step, holding up a white rhododendron.

"Hey up, kiddo!" he grinned in a friendly manner. "What you doin' with that?"

"I'm selling it. The British Legion sent me. They need the money to help the wounded soldiers". It could have been Ernie talking. He would have been proud of me.

"Hey, Mam! Come and look at this!" the soldier shouted into the living room, and laughed loudly.

It seemed as if the whole family responded to his call, crowding into the narrow hall. They stood there staring at me, laughing and giggling as I shuffled in torment on the step. I must have interrupted a party judging by the glasses of beer most of them were clutching.

"What's he selling?" a middle-aged woman asked testily.

"The British Legion's sent him with some flowers to sell for wounded soldiers," the soldier explained. The whole crowd of them laughed at me.

"I bet he's nicked 'em," somebody said.

"D'you want one, Mam?" the soldier asked of the middle-aged woman.

"I've got enough flowers in me own front garden," the woman said dismissively.

"A young woman pushed to the front. "They're lovely," she exclaimed, and delicately picked one out of my box. "They don't need this," she said pulling off the silver foil around it.

"Do you want it?" the soldier asked. He slipped his arm around the young woman's waist.

"Please," she said.

The soldier gave me sixpence, although I hadn't told him how much they were. He winked at me, then closed the door. I was going to ask him what regiment he was in as he wore blue trousers with his khaki shirt. I could hear the continuing laughter from inside, and thought it best not to disturb them again.

I found Mo sitting disconsolately on the kerb further up Withern Road, his box by his side, and still full. He was picking a rhododendron to pieces and flicking the bits into the gutter.

"How much you made?" I asked, pleased with myself.

"Nowt," he grumbled. "They all told me to bogger off."

Mo's failure as a salesman only sweetened my own rare success. We walked back to Ernie's house, kicking the blooms out of Mo's box over people's privet hedges. I hadn't told Mo that I'd made nearly two shillings. Ernie was having his tea when we got back. He came out of the house with a chunk of fruit cake in his fist.

"Did you mek owt?" he asked without seeming particularly interested.

"Eightpence," I lied in the best Ernie style.

"Nowt," Mo grunted sullenly. He eyed Ernie's nob of cake. "I'm going home for me tea." He left the back garden, thoroughly disgruntled.

Ernie gazed down at my forlorn blooms wilting in the box. "They're dying," he said without feeling.

"Did you sell any?" I demanded.

"Nah. I didn't bother. Our Dad gave me five bob when he came home pissed from the Legion. You can keep that eightpence if you want."

"What're you gonna do with all these flowers, then?" Mo had left his box on the doorstep.

Ernie thought for a moment, biting into his cake. Then his mam called from the living-room for him to come in and finish his tea. "Aw, sod it," he said without passion, then picked up the boxes and tipped their fragile contents into the dustbin. "See you tomorrow," he said, and slammed the back door.

Mam never asked how I got to the Forum that night. She must have assumed that I'd fiddled her change again. She did look a bit pleased when I offered her one of the fresher rhododendrons rescued from Ernie's dustbin. "Mam, d'you know what regiment in the army wears blue trousers instead of khaki ones," I asked before I went to bed.

"That'll be the hospital uniform," she explained. "It's what all the wounded soldiers wear."

104

Chapter 14

The Redcaps are Coming

A photograph of Cousin Tommy shows him unusually serious in his sailor's uniform. He is dressed for guard duty, shouldering a rifle at the camp gate. He stands rigidly to attention, obviously proud of himself as he stares meanly into the camera. A youth dressed to kill. On leave, he brings home another photograph, a postcard of his first ship, a destroyer cutting through the waves. He is proud of that, too, and gives it to me to stick on the bedroom wall.

After a few months, the destroyer is sunk by a torpedo. Tommy is sent home after being picked up out of the sea. This time he is quieter, the serious look permanent, his cockiness changed to surly aggression which only Aunt Liz can forgive. The youth has become a man.

He goes to sea again in another destroyer. In the Mediterranean the ship is machine-gunned and bombed by an Italian plane which kills his mates on a pom-pom gun. Finally, he is transferred to an armed merchantman as a gunner. He likes this ship because the captain gets him off a charge when he is arrested for skipping ashore to fight in a professional boxing tournament. This ship, also, is sunk and Tommy sees the captain die in the water.

Home on leave after being rescued once more, Tommy hardly speaks to anyone, not even to his mother. Once he entertained me with stories about the ships he served on. Now he ignores me, and never mentions the navy. I don't know this new, brooding Tommy and soon lose interest in him. When his leave is finished he doesn't go back, but sits at our table in hunch introspection, drinking mugs of tea. He gets on the women's nerves, and his unpredictable temper flares into bouts of sustained swearing which upsets Aunt Mabel and

Mam. Sometimes he visits Aunt Ida's house on Hyson Green, and she also complains about his surly depression. I think they are all a bit afraid of him.

One night he is in a pub on Hyson Green with Mam and her sisters when a lone American soldier walks in. The G.I. is a quiet-looking bloke in glasses, Mam reports that Tommy suddenly jumps up as the G.I. passes their table on his way to the bar and hits him, knocking him unconscious, his cap and his glasses flying across the room. Mam and Aunt Ida help to bring the G.I. round, retrieve his cap and his broken glasses, over which he weeps, then get him to his feet.

When Aunt Ida arrives home, Tommy is fast asleep on her new sofa, a sacred object no member of the family is allowed to sit on. She kicks Tommy out, and he is ostracised by the rest of the family as a contemptible figure. On the run from the military police, he gets a job driving a lorry for a coal merchant who used to watch him box. Gradually, Tommy is accepted back into the family fold for the sake of Aunt Liz who is desperately worried about him. Just when it seems as if the police will never catch him, and he will spend the rest of the war delivering coal for the friendly coal merchant, they surprise him in his lodgings, chase him up the stairs and catch him struggling to escape out of a bedroom window. I see Aunt Liz cry for the first time when she is told that he is handcuffed and still fighting as the police drag him into their van.

* * *

Uncle George, Tommy's dad, was fed up of the army after he lost his French-Canadian pal. He settled in our house with Aunt Liz after one week-end leave, changed into his old flannel trousers and sports jacket, fitted his flat cap on his greying head and strolled out to look for some casual, no-questions-asked labouring work. While he was out one day the redcaps, as the military police were called for obvious reasons, surrounded our house – two at the front door, and two at the back. Both pairs banged hard on the doors as though that would flush Uncle George out. Mam opened the front door to stop them because our neighbour's curtains were flapping in anticipation of some excitement. The moment Mam opened a gap in the front door two redcaps dashed into the hall, pushing her aside. They stomped upstairs in their steel-shod boots. I could hear the living-room light-fitting rattle as they clattered from one bedroom to another. Aunt Liz was agitated, moaning low as she poked the fire unnecessarily, doing her best to appear normal in the circumstances.

The boots clomped back downstairs, more slowly this time. "Where is he?" a sergeant demanded in the menacing tone of the policeman.

"I don't know," Aunt Liz said as calmly as she was able. "He ent been here, and that's a fact." She glanced across at Mam. "He ent been here, has he Ada?"

"No," Mam said. "We don't know where he is. We haven't seen him."

"Then what's his kit-bag doing upstairs? You're not helping him by lying. Tell him to report back. He'll only make it worse for himself." He paused, looking at Mam and Aunt Liz as though he felt sorry for them. "Tell him not to be stupid," he said. "He can't get away with it."

The redcaps disappeared as quickly as they had arrived. Aunt Liz gave one of her little moans, shaking her head in agitation. "By christ, don't I have summat to put with with!" she wailed, the mother and wife of deserters.

"I don't know what the neighbours think," Mam said. She was angry. I guessed that what really troubled her was how Dad would react if he found out that we had been raided by redcaps.

"I'll swing for him one of these days!" Aunt Liz threatened, regaining her composure.

Uncle George laughed dismissively when he heard Aunt Liz's emotional account of her fright. "They waint catch me," he boasted. "They've got too many young 'uns on the run to bother with me."

"You're going back tomorrow," Aunt Liz declared. "We'll all finish up in the clink if you don't!"

"No I'm not." Uncle George slurped his tea from his saucer in his usual manner. "If they want me they'll have to catch me first. They're all pig-thick."

I didn't really know what had made him fed up with the army. He conveyed little of what he was thinking. Nobody really knew him very well. He was a law unto himself, and Authority was the enemy he needed to be one step ahead of. He was probably no more than bored after he lost his French-Canadian pal. Too old to be a front-line soldier, he could make the conflict more exciting by making it personal: Uncle George versus the Army. The danger from the redcaps brought a glint to his eye, set his tomahawk face in its stoniest expression. I thought I could understand why Cousin Tommy had deserted; but his father was always a mystery to me.

Mam didn't openly betray her own feelings about harbouring a deserter in the house, she was loyal to her eldest sister, always. But I knew she resented the burden imposed on her. Aunt Mabel had been spared having to witness the intrusion of the redcaps, and the latent violence implicit in their dash upstairs. She was out at the time, but Mam's account frightened her. Living with her sisters had begun to pall for her, because it meant having to put up with their families, too. Shortly after the incident, she went down to the corporation housing office to enquire about a council house for herself. In a matter of weeks, she moved out of Frinton Road with her posh bedroom suite to take up the tenancy of a house in Bilborough.

Uncle George, meanwhile, was confident that the redcaps wouldn't bother him again. The generals wouldn't miss one elderly private in the Pioneer Corps, would they? He spent more time lounging in our living-room, swigging tea from his saucer and puffing on his Woodbines. He gave me orders to keep an eye open for policemen and redcaps, and to report to him on the double if I spotted any suspicious looking vehicles. At first it was exciting to be a look-out, scanning the street for the redcaps to round the corner. I turned it into a game of cowboys and Apaches, then into spies and Nazis. Finally, I found myself counting how many people went down the road, and how many people went up. When the futility of this became clear – just as many people went up the road as went down it – I gave up being a look-out and went off to find my pals. My desertion didn't seem to worry Uncle George, he was so cocky now he had taken to sunning himself at the front gate, smoking and chatting to neighbours as though he had nothing to hide.

It came as quite a surprise to him, therefore, when a redcap wagon screeched to a halt outside the house while he was inside enjoying a leisurely breakfast. A posse of redcaps dashed up the garden path before he could move. "Christ – it's the redcaps!" Aunt Liz shouted. Her warning made Uncle George leap from his chair and sprint up the stairs. The redcaps came through the open back door and into the living room. They heard rapid footsteps on the stairs and clattered after him before he could reach the top. The redcaps must have run into the wrong bedroom because Uncle George evaded them, racing back downstairs again, the redcaps yelling after him. Frantically, he wrestled with the lock on the front door as Aunt Liz moaned in tribulation and Ida clung to her. "What're they doing to me Dad?" my cousin squealed.

The redcaps tumbled downstairs just as Uncle George managed to open the front door, only to dash into the arms of another redcap, his face set in a regulation scowl. Together, they bundled him down the path to the waiting wagon, his arms twisted up his back. Uncle George managed to glance over his shoulder. "Ta-ra!" he yelled as they threw him into the back of the wagon. Before any of us could recover from the shock Uncle George was driven off. The whole incident had taken no more than a couple of minutes, and Uncle George's breakfast was still warm on its plate.

The shame of having the redcaps invade the house once again put a strain on the relationship between Mam and Aunt Liz. Mam went quiet, Aunt Liz understanding well enough that her sister's silence was an unspoken complaint against the humiliation. Nothing was actually said. The sisters might argue with husbands, neighbours, and even their children, but they would never argue with each other. Aunt Liz knew, however, that she had outstayed her welcome and departed with Ida to live in a flat close to Hyson Green. They didn't have to wait too long for Uncle George to return to them. He was discharged from the army, presumably as a lost cause.

When Dad came home on leave and learned about Uncle George's capture he was amused, a response which surprised me. He thought his brother-in-law a "character", and regarded his exploits with what I suspect was a sneaking admiration, the attraction of opposites, perhaps. Of Tommy's desertion he was totally contemptuous. "He's yellow," he snapped. "He's all mouth and no guts!"

I thought it was a rotten thing to say about someone who had been torpedoed twice, machine-gunned from the air, and rescued from the sea. I don't think Dad would ever desert, though, even in extremis. He was too conscious of showing a respectable face to the world, no matter what went on inside the house. His deference to Authority was itself a kind of cowardice: the inadequate father and bullying husband was a Good Citizen to the world outside. Humble before his own father, deferential to people higher up the social ladder than himself, he had no patience with those who rebelled. As far as he was concerned, desertion was cowardice, but his lack of charity only served to re-establish Cousin Tommy in my esteem.

* * *

I hadn't seen the last of the redcaps with the undignified exit of Uncle George in their custody. The next time I saw them they were chasing strangers, and not my relatives. Brenda noticed them first when she was playing in the front garden. In she ran, quivering in breathless excitement, a little afraid. "There's a load of soldiers jumping over fences down the road – come and look!" she piped. Mam and I dashed to the front window for a grandstand view. Sure enough, the redcaps were in action again. About half-a-dozen of them were racing up and down the paths and entries of houses lower down the street, obviously in pursuit of a quarry we couldn't see. Judging by the way the redcaps were methodically working their way up the street, they couldn't see him either. With awesome athleticism they performed one-armed vaults over privet hedges and garden gates shouting hoarse and urgent instructions to each other. A whistle was blown, and suddenly the redcaps converged on a single entry leading to the back garden of a woman we called "News of the World" because she always had an interesting fund of low-life gossip to report. "They must've got the poor sod," Mam said.

It had been exciting while it lasted, but the action was all too brief to lift the boredom on what was a dull afternoon. I picked up a book, but couldn't get into it, tossing it aside. The incident had triggered the desire for a more adventurous activity, perhaps in the company of

Ernie and Mo. "I'm going down to Ernie's," I informed Mam. "I'll be back at tea-time."

Opening the back door, I stepped into the porch, slipping on my jacket. I thought I heard a sound from inside the lavatory, the door of which faced the back door. It was a slight, indefinable noise, something like breathing. I paused for a moment, listening and wondering if I dare open the lavatory door. But I didn't have to do anything. The door opened slowly from inside and two half-dressed soldiers stared out at me, both of them panting heavily. If I hadn't been rigid with shock I would have run, but one of the soldiers winked and I felt a bit more at ease. He was dark haired and sported a Clark Gable moustache. He put a finger to his lips to indicate that I shouldn't speak, then he reached out to drop his other hand on my shoulder and yanked me into the lavatory, closing the door on us. Both men were without shoes and jackets, their khaki trousers held up by braces.

"Have you seen any redcaps around?" Clark Gable asked. His tone was conspiratorial, as though I was invited to join the game of hide-and-seek they were playing.

"They ran down an entry on the other side of the street," I told him, glad to be of help. "I think they've jumped over the backs into Woodfield Road."

The two soldiers looked at each other and nodded. "Don't be scared," Clark Gable said, forcing a smile.

"I'm not," I declared, truthfully. "The redcaps got my uncle a few weeks ago." The information was intended to make it plain that I was on their side. Clark Gable grinned.

"Who else lives here?"

"Me Mam and me sister."

"Not your dad?" the other soldier asked. He hadn't said a word until then. His breath was whistling through his nostrils as though he was totally puffed. He looked more nervous than Clark Gable.

"Me dad's in the army. He's in the Royal Horse Artillery." I was beginning to enjoy the new lease of life they gave to the afternoon.

"Ask your mam to come out here," Clark Gable said with a lightness that suggested there was no risk involved.

I did as I was told, trotting into the living room where Mam was ironing. "I thought you was going out to play?" she said without looking up.

"I was, but there's two soldiers in the lav. The redcaps are after them. They want to see you."

Mam plonked the iron down. "Trust 'em to come here! Don't I have some bloody luck, eh? If it's not your Uncle George being chased, it's some bogger I don't even know."

"One of them looks just like Clark Gable," I added, hoping it might make the situation less fraught.

"I'll bloody Clark Gable him!" Mam threatened, then marched through the kitchen and into the porch. The two soldiers had stepped out of the lavatory and had lit cigarettes.

"What the hell's going off?" Mam demanded. "I've got kids in the house." When she said that I knew she was scared. Brenda was still in the front garden, but might come running in if she heard voices at the back. "I don't want redcaps here again."

Clark Gable offered Mam a cigarette, which she took. "Sorry, duck." he said, offering her a light. "Let us just finish this fag then we'll be off."

The sight of them, shoeless, tousled and lost looking must have eased Mam's initial fear, won her sympathy. "As long as you don't come in the house," she said, relieved to find them so friendly. "Where're you from?"

"Just off Withern Road," Clark Gable explained. "We had to jump out of the bedroom window. We've jumped every fence between our road and this. Talk about the Grand National! Can you see the redcaps anywhere?"

Mam stepped out of the porch into the back garden. "There's nothing out here." She shivered, although it was a mild afternoon. "Go and look on the front, Del," she ordered. "And tell Bren to stay in the garden."

I ran to the front of the house, climbing on the gate to search the street. "I'm going to tell Mam you're climbing," Brenda said, automatically critical of my behaviour, then went on with her doll game. I was Geronimo, steely eyes searching out the U.S. cavalry. I was Errol Flynn scanning the horizon from his pirate ship. Mrs Hancock, our local misery, was complaining loudly to a neighbour about footprints in her borders. A toddler was sitting on a kerb poking a cane down a grate. I listened for sirens, gunshots, screams, but all I heard were distant shouts from a game of football, or a fight. I jumped off the gate, whipped my horse, Trigger, into a gallop and returned to Mam and the soldiers.

"The coast is clear," I reported.

"That's a good lad," Clark Gable said. He patted me on the shoulder. He was the sort I wouldn't have minded having as a dad.

"You'd better push off," Mam said, only it was an order, one which Clark Gable seemed to understand, and acknowledged with a strained sort of smile. "Thanks," he said.

"Yeah, thanks," his pal said bleakly.

Mam retreated into the kitchen. "Good luck," she said. I hung back hoping for more scouting duties before they went, but Mam dug her fingers into my arm and dragged me after her. "That hurt!" I protested.

"Get inside," she snapped. She was shivering as though she'd felt a sudden cold draught. She turned the key in the back door lock, turning it slowly to minimise the sound. I raced upstairs, kneeling on the bedroom window-sill to observe the soldiers departure. Clark Gable was balancing on the top of an old, upturned bucket, trying to peek over the hedges of neighbouring gardens. He stepped down then signalled to his pal. Both men struggled over our hedge and fell into Mrs Peach's garden which had an entry into Bradfield Road, a route which could lead them out of the estate. I pushed the bedroom window open, expecting to hear a hue and cry start up immediately. There was only the muffled bass of a radio or radiogram playing a Bing Crosby record, the plaintive whine of a dog that sounded locked in. A cabbage white butterfly fluttered in broken flight over our weed-filled vegetable patch, but finding no cabbages, flew away.

* * *

Several weeks later I was sauntering home with Mam's *Evening Post*, reading through it as I always did, when I spotted a news story which set my heart thumping. I ran the rest of the way home to show the story to Mam. Two deserters from the Sherwood Foresters, one of them from Withern Road, Broxtowe, had hit a railway guard with a length of piping before stealing mailbags from a train standing in Victoria Station. The two thieves had been chased and captured by police, but only after one of the officers was injured. Both soldiers were sentenced to five years hard labour at the Assizes. Mam nearly passed out when she read the story. "Christ almighty! They could've done us in – they were dangerous! It's a good job your Dad don't know, and don't you tell him. I don't know, don't I have some luck, eh?"

I couldn't see how they had been bad luck, or even dangerous. They seemed okay to me, well, Clark Gable did. But the quiet one was a bit funny looking. He might have hit us with a length of piping if Clark Gable hadn't been there. I felt sorry for Clark. He'd seemed a nice bloke to me. But feeling sorry for the wrong sort of people seemed to be a weakness I was lumbered with. I know what Clark did was rotten, and it's something Dad would never do. But *he* had his own way of hurting people.

Chapter 15

Nineteen Forty-Three

Mam's brief period of affluence ended when she had to give up her job making bullets at the Raleigh Cycle factory because she was pregnant – evidence that Dad's leaves were more peaceful now that the sisters and their families had left Frinton Road. By this time I had learned how pregnancies were caused. It was a biological fact I found hard to believe at first, but Ernie assured me it was true. Although it shocked me, I came to realize that there was more to Mam and Dad's relationship than I could fathom. Between the arguments there was something else going on, but it embarrassed me to think about it, although I was relieved by the thought that they might have cared for each other in ways I hadn't suspected.

The loss of her job, though, made Mam poor again. Her complaint that she couldn't manage on a soldier's pay began once more. She was far from extravagant: we had no luxuries, not even the radio I longed for, nor did she spend much on herself. Her army allowance slipped through her fingers with little in the way of comfort to show for it. She spent the allowance on the basic necessities of rationed food, fuel, and on trying to keep down the rent arrears. When Mam's purse was completely empty she borrowed from her sisters, but that meant she was hard-pressed to pay her way through the following week. She had fallen into the credit trap of buying all our clothes and household goods on "tick". The need for new sheets, towels or crockery meant an extra credit "cheque" was taken out. Eventually it became impossible for her to pay back all she owed to sisters, shops and tallymen. Trying to satisfy them all was an unsuccessful juggling act: if she paid the rent the tallyman would go away empty handed. If she paid the tallyman the rent arrears would grow longer, and letters threatening eviction would arrive to torment her.

One of my increasing load of domestic duties was to forestall the mild-mannered tallyman who tried to collect the weekly payment on the goods purchased from his firm's warehouse.

"He's coming!" she would whisper hoarsely whenever she saw him hurry up the garden path, for she was always wary when a debt collector was due. "Tell him I'm not in."

"I told him that last week," I would protest. I was always embarrassed when I had to stutter my way through the obvious lie.

"Do as you're told. Tell him I'll make it right with him next week."

On one of his fruitless calls, I made the classic gaffe: "Me mam says she's not in," I mumbled stupidly to the irritated tallyman.

"That's what she says, is it?" he said wryly, scribbling in his bulging payment book. "Well you tell her it's three weeks owing, and I'm getting fed up with it."

"You silly bogger!" Mam snorted when I slouched back to the living room where she had been listening, although she couldn't help laughing in spite of being incensed by the tallyman's weak protest. "*He's* getting fed up with it, is he? He wants to have this lot – he'd be fed up then!"

Mam's first priority was buying the weekly food ration. The provision of food came before any clamour for money by debt collectors, the rent man, or even by Aunt Mabel. The second essential was a fire in the grate, a comfort which was hard to achieve sometimes as fuel was in short supply, or there was no cash to pay for it. One desperately cold winter's day, with deep snow on the ground, we watched the embers of a dying fire sink into the bottom of the grate to generate nothing but smoke. "Are you sure there's no more coal?" Mam asked. I had swept the floor of the kitchen coalhouse to collect just enough "slack" for even this spiritless fire. "There's only dust," I shivered. "Have a look yourself."

"What're we going to do? We can't go all day without a fire."

The coalman wouldn't deliver until the next day, and the snow might prevent even that delivery. We would have to beg a few lumps from someone to keep us going until then.

116

"You'll have to go down to your Auntie Edie's," Mam said. "Take the pram, and tell her I'll let her have it back when the coalman's been. Tell her we haven't got a fire."

Deep snow had drifted into the open porch, almost blocking the back door. I got the dustpan and cleared it before leaving on my errand. Mam came out to watch me. "You'll be frozen before you start," she said, and she was right.

I straightened my back and jabbed the dustpan into the heap of snow I had piled onto the garden. Cold had penetrated my bad right foot, making it throb. Mam stood with her arms folded in her apron, shivering at the edge of the porch. She was staring hard at the back of the Whiting's house which stood at an angle to ours. "Look at that!" she said. There was a light in her eye which I knew well enough: it was the hard glint of the gambler, the look of triumph in the eye when a certainty has been spotted. The door of the Whiting's outside coalhouse was swinging wide, blown open by last night's blizzard, no doubt. Inside were piled huge lumps of coal, enough to last a household for weeks. The curtains were still drawn on the sleeping house. The whole neighbourhood was silent under the snow. "They wouldn't miss one lump," Mam said, nodding towards the coalhouse. "Go and fetch one, Del. They won't miss it."

"No!" I protested. The idea of stealing it came as a shock. Mam, and Dad, were as honest as the day was long. Stealing was anathema to them both. The only person in our house who stole, occasionally, was me, and that was usually something to eat like an apple from the greengrocers.

"Go on," Mam urged. "Nobody'll see you."

"It's stealing," I protested weakly.

"It's bleddy cold, an'all," Mam said, and I realized how desperate the cold had made her. The Whitings didn't speak to us, considering themselves superior to most of the neighbours. I don't know why, except that they didn't speak with such obvious Nottingham accents as most people on Frinton Road. People on the road had quickly arranged their own social pecking order for whatever reason, probably one based on the same kind of self-deception that made Mr and Mrs Whiting believe that they were better than anybody else.

I knew it would give Mam particular satisfaction to use a lump of Mrs Whiting's coal on our fire.

I thought of the freezing temperature in the living-room. At least I would return from Aunt Edie's to a warm fire. I blew on my fingers, then nervously trudged through the snow to the privet hedge which divided our house from the Whiting's. The hedge was so sparse in its winter dearth that I was able to push through it with ease. I glanced up at the drawn curtains at the Whiting's bedrooms, then ploughed through their snow to the coalhouse in an absolute silence. I lifted up a huge lump of coal so heavy it hurt the muscles of my back when I tried to walk with it. My ears were cocked for a sudden shout of protest and accusation from one of the bedroom windows as I struggled, doubled up with the effort, back across the Whiting's garden. I heaved the lump through the privet hedge, climbed through the gap I had made then had to lift the lump out of the drift into which I'd tossed it before scrambling back to our kitchen coalhouse. Mam's eyes were shining now – whether with delight at having coal again, or because she had put one over on the snooty Mrs Whiting, I couldn't be sure. "Pass me the hammer!" she crowed in triumph.

As I forced Peter's delapidated old pram through the deep snow on the path to fetch more coal from Aunt Edie's, I could hear the happy cracks of Mam's hammer smashing the Whiting's lump into convenient pieces. It was only when I glanced across to the Whiting's rear that I noticed the gap I had made in the hedge, and worse, the deeply-trodden footsteps in the snow which led with tell-tale directness from the gap to the coalhouse. But that was Mam's problem now, and Mrs Whiting was scared of her, anyway.

* * *

The scarcity of fuel for domestic fires meant that queuing for it became another chore, superseding queuing for corned-beef as the most hateful of all chores. On Saturday mornings, in the worst of the weather, a local coal-merchant drove his lorry onto a patch of cinder-covered wasteground behind the Forum Cinema. He served the shivering queue by emptying his bags of coal and coke into the crude, home-made barrows, old prams and pushchairs which made up the ramshackle convoy that had waited with grumbling impatience for an hour. Nobody liked using coke because there were few flames when it burned, and that didn't seem like a proper fire. I utilized Peter's old pram as a conveyance. Its wheels had buckled under the strain of its being used to carry coal and coke.

If the coal-merchant failed to arrive with his load, the disgruntled queue behind the Forum broke up, most of us setting out like the procession of Belgian refugees for the Basford gasworks, two miles away. Sometimes I pushed on directly to the gasworks as I could always be sure of collecting my load of coke there. On such occasions, Mam sent Brenda with me to help push the heavy load. My sister hated the task even more than I did. She lacked the strength to be of much use pushing the pram's dead weight. When the frost bit her fingers it only added to her misery, and she would cry even though she was usually braver, and far less inclined to tears than I was. Only the collapse of the pram into a heap of useless junk saved us, ultimately, from the Saturday morning ordeal, although its final journey was purgatory for us.

I complained to Mam that the pram, now in a state of advanced dilapidation, would not survive another four miles fully loaded, especially as it would have to be pushed through the snow which had fallen in the night. Mam considered my gloomy prediction a crafty ploy to get out of the errand, so off we trudged, my sister and I accusing each other of not doing a fair share of the pushing. The journey through the snow-blocked streets was difficult enough with an empty pram: one wheel kept falling off every few yards and needed sliding back onto the axle with stiff, frozen fingers. By the time we reached the gasworks the queue was a hundred yards long. Brenda and I were snapping at each other in bad temper, fingers, feet and noses aching with cold. We shuffled forward in the queue inches at a time until we reached the front. It had taken an hour of shivering misery in the dirty slush of the gasworks yard.

If the journey with an empty pram was difficult, the return trip with the heavy load of coke spilling out was a nightmare. The loose wheel rolled off into the slush before we reached the gate which took us out of the gasworks yard. The chassis of the pram was sitting on the axles, making it almost impossible to lift when we had to negotiate a kerb. The snow had compacted under people's feet, and was freezing, which made the pram slide sideways. Brenda was so cold she was crying all the time. Eventually we reached softer snow and the pram became easier to push, although the loose wheel rolled off after a few revolutions. Finally, in a raging temper, I hurled the wheel violently across the road with a terrible swear word I had never used before. Fortunately, Brenda was lost so deep in her own despair that she didn't hear it, and the obscenity would go unreported. The wheel was sticking out of a snow drift, a mocking reminder of the predicament I was now in.

After half a mile of hopeless floundering, I discovered that it was easier to push the pram on three reasonably straight wheels. It began to run straight. I had to lift as well as push forward: lift, push, rest, lift, push, rest. Slowly I made progress, with Brenda disappearing into the distance ahead after abandoning all pretence that she was helping me. Few people were on the streets, and those that were passed me with a pitying look, or pretended that they hadn't seen me in case I asked them for help. My only consolation was that the pram was now a complete wreck. I promised myself I would take pleasure in kicking it to pieces when I got back to Frinton Road. I would make sure that it would never carry coke again.

Mam was peering out of the window when I reached our house, forewarned by Brenda's arrival before me. I was wet, frozen and exhausted. I was expecting a welcoming fuss, a cup of tea and a kind word after I peeled my frozen fingers from the steel pram handle. But she was too dismayed by the condition of the pram to dish out tea or accolades as a reward for my epic journey. "Look at the state of it!" she whinged as she surveyed the wreck. "What're we going to do now? I don't know, it's one bleddy thing after another. Don't I have some luck!"

* * *

As a faithful believer in those twin deities, Good Luck and Bad Luck, it was logical that Mam should be a devoted follower of horse racing. Betting on a horse at Newmarket or Epsom expressed her faith that the unlucky star under which she had been born would take pity on her and move to another part of the sky. One day, soon, Chance would intervene to solve all her financial problems with one big win. Down to her last shilling, she would stake it all on an outsider in the hope that her Good Luck angel was on form, and would provide. She scribbled her bets on scraps of paper, sometimes on an end-paper from one of my library books. If it was a "big race" such as the Derby or the 2,000 Guineas she would use a sheet of the Basildon Bond she used to write to Dad. I always used rational arguments against her skinning herself completely when she didn't even have enough money to pay the rent. As I was doing this when I was about twelve years old it didn't cut much ice with her, and she told me to mind my own business. "Run with this to Brady's!" she would order. "Don't dawdle because there's a horse in the two o'clock race." Brady had a hairdressing shop on Aspley Lane, but he was also an illegal bookie whose wife took bets at the back door. I fumed at the daftness of risking what little we had, but sense is irrelevant to a gambler: they trust in instinct, the hunches that having nothing to do with reason. Occasionally she won a few shillings, but her method of selection was so unscientific that I wasn't troubled with the chore of collecting her winnings very often.

Mam's first principle of betting was that the favourite was there to be beaten. This prejudice against likely winners was induced by her particular dislike of the great jockey, Gordon Richards, whom she loathed because he always rode the favourites which beat her selections. The way to make a fortune, she thought, was to find a nag of unfulfilled promise, at odds of about 20-1, which might pull off a surprise. Three dark-horses doing it on the same day would be the miracle she was waiting for. A grey horse stood a good chance of winning as it was a lucky colour. If a horse had been placed several times without actually pushing its nose first past the post, then Fate ordained that its time must be due. Unfortunately, Fate didn't often perform as expected, and Mam swore when "Big Head" as she called the monotonously successful Richards, upset her psychic reading of the runners and riders in the form page of the *Daily Express*. Horses with names which revived a memory of something she had dreamed were also scribbled down as though they were coded messages from our dead relatives: "I was dreaming about our Jack last night," she would say, and off I would go with a shilling bet on some equestrian cripple named "Jack's the Lad" or "Applejack". Her favourite bet was an each-way treble, when she could afford it. But its success relied upon such an awesome effort from Good Luck on her behalf that the results always brought a curse on Gordon Richard's parentage, and on his future as a jockey.

It was many years before Mam got to attend a race meeting, and she loved the spectacle. By that time, though, her children had grown up and she was financially secure in middle age. She still enjoyed a gamble, her hope of the big win transferred to Littlewoods Football Pools. She still employed the same principles of superstitious belief that it was only a matter of time before her teasing Lucky Star shone on her as recompense for her hardship. "I've got a funny feeling about the pools this week," she would say as she carefully drew her crosses. "My brother Arthur spoke to me in a dream last night. I could see him plain as day ..."

* * *

The Winter and Spring of 1943 had been a cold, discouraging period for all of us. But Summer and Autumn ushered in better days for me, if not for Mam. The sirens rarely sounded now: the war receded into the distance for a time. I still followed its progress in the newspapers. The Russians had become my new heroes, and Uncle Joe Stalin was a cuddly idol, revered almost as much as Winston Churchill.

My sister, Valerie, was born – a rather frail baby, perhaps because of our restricted diet. Being the eldest child, nearly twelve years old, I was regarded by Mam as a surrogate adult until Dad returned to resume his authority – a situation which Brenda resented, and never really accepted, and rightly so for she was far more responsible and level-headed than me. I had to grow up fast. But it meant I had more freedom and independence without the discipline that Dad would have imposed. My position in the family made me somewhat arrogant and cheeky, at least according to my aunts, and to Brenda – and they were probably right.

122

In contrast to the new baby, Peter was a robust, energetic and healthy toddler, a rather shy four-year old who followed me everywhere. He loved being out in the fields and woods of Strelley and Bilborough where he picked up my bad habits of bird nesting, scrumping for apples, pears and damsons, and trespassing. He was strong and fearless for his age, although his toddler legs were a liability when we had to make a quick getaway from farmers and their dogs. Rural enemies of lads from the estate, these country folk and their animals would inflict actual physical hurt on us if we were foolish enough to get caught. In summer, when the heat had made us lazy, we were content to swish our sticks at nettle heads, or lie back in the long grass to watch the frantic buzzing around a wasp's nest we had tried to dig out for its grubs, precious bait for Ernie when he fancied an hour of fishing in the Wollaton canal. I enjoyed having Peter with me. Together we would chase richly patterned butterflies, try to throw our jackets over them, or simply watch strange looking beetles run through their grass jungle or crawl on our hands. Ernie complained about my "dragging a kid" with us. But Peter's fascination with the new world he was discovering just beyond the unlovely, repetitive roads of the estate was reward enough for having to look after my brother.

That summer was made all the sweeter for my having seen the last of Mr Alkman and his intimidated cohorts in the junior school. In September I walked through the gates of the senior school feeling pretty grown up, with the optimistic anticipation that comes with a fresh start. I joined the new boys crowding into the impressive school hall with its wine-coloured drapes, its wide stage over which hung the Player School logo: an image of two trees and the letters "JP". Nobody knew what the two trees meant. When we settled we were greeted by the headmaster, Ernest Martin who stood beneath the logo, grinning in amusement, perhaps because we looked scared to death. Somehow I knew, perhaps instinctively, that I was going to like him, and his school.

My new form teacher was Mr Sadler, dapper in his grey suit, a gold watch chain hanging across his waistcoat. A tubby little man in middle age, he was strict, but had retained a sense of humour in spite of a long working life teaching elementary schoolboys. There were 45 of us in his class, and he treated us all with equal fairness. He told us that his passion for cricket had stopped him from going mad. A good cricketer in his day – or so he told us – he reported his son's score and bowling figures every Monday morning. Proud that Sadler junior was even better than he had been, he was overjoyed when the young man played a game or two for Notts second eleven. Mr Sadler exuded quiet authority. Occasionally he would express his exasperation with a slow boy by throwing a piece of chalk at him, but usually, a word was enough to control us, for we respected him not only for his fairness, but because we knew that he worked hard for us, the methodical, patient manner of his teaching a welcome contrast to the cruder methods we suffered in the junior school. I enjoyed his English lessons. We read poetry aloud, memorized it, performed it. My interest in the sound and rhythm of language was nurtured in that crowded classroom, never to leave me. I was picked out as the "reader" of the class and was chosen to recite John Masefield's *Cargoes* from memory in front of the whole school during morning assembly. I was so panic-stricken with stage fright that I toyed with the idea of playing truant for the day, but remembered the sneers of the schoolboard man, and thought better of it. My classmates were already ribbing me on the way to school so that by the time I had to climb the steps to the hall stage, my face was burning in embarrassment.

> *Quinquireme of Nineveh from distant Ophir,*
> *Rowing home to haven in sunny Palestine,*
> *With a cargo of ivory,*
> *And apes and peacocks*
> *Sandalwood, cedarwood and sweet white wine ...*

My pals sniggered on cue, stuffing their fists or handkerchiefs into their mouths to stop themselves from snorting in audible amusement. Afterwards they told me gleefully that I had looked comically serious as I intoned each tricky line with ridiculous precision, my mouth opening and closing as though I was a fish.

For what must have been the first time since infant school, I wrote stories – scrawled, blot-stained narratives of violent adventure with dialogue remembered from films I had seen at the Forum. My rambling work brought looks of surprise, and amusement, to Mr Sadler's face. He nodded in approbation in spite of his complaints about my bad handwriting.

I was interested in history, too, responding to the enthusiasm of our teacher, Miss Balfour, fresh out of university. A plain, dumpy young woman who still wore her dashing, multi-coloured college blazer, she showed her excitement by exclaiming "gosh!" and "golly!" – words I thought only characters in public-school stories used. Interesting as she made it, history wasn't quite as fascinating as Miss Balfour herself. Sometimes she would dance around the classroom in high spirits, her eyes sparkling with some inner happiness. On other days she might burst into tears inexplicably, then run out with a sob. Mr Martin would take her place, sometimes annoyed, sometimes amused by her histrionics. We couldn't understand such behaviour until a more worldly boy pointed out that her moods were connected in some way with her trips to the woodwork stockroom. We began a more careful watch on her. Yes – she *did* sneak into the stockroom at lunchtime, her head held low as if ashamed. Fortunately there was a door in the corridor which opened onto the stockroom. A few boys were bold enough to squint through the keyhole. One or two said they had seen Miss Balfour standing pretty close to the obnoxious woodwork teacher, Mr Curle, engrossed in intimate-looking conversations. One or two of older boys reported that they had seen more physical intimacies, but we didn't believe it because the older boys were always pretending they knew somebody who had had sex. It was hard for us to imagine that Miss Balfour and Mr Curle could be having a romance, let alone having sex. Both were quite ugly in our eyes. Surely you had to look like Errol Flynn and Claudette Colbert for "romance" to flourish? Miss Balfour was a good teacher, and we liked her: but who would want to stroke her breasts? And the idea that any woman, even a plain one, could cry over the bald, middle-aged, bad-tempered and sarcastic woodwork teacher was beyond belief. Adult love was a mystery, although it added a bit of spice to our history lessons.

The humane regime of the Player School was ruled by Mr Martin with firmness, yet with a humour which made him easily approachable. He didn't try to make us afraid of him. We obeyed most of the rules because we *wanted* to please him. "My mother called me Ernest because she wanted me to be earnest," he told us one day with a wry grin. "I'm afraid I may have let her down." He may have disappointed his mother, but he never let us down.

* * *

At home, we ended the year as poor as we began it. Its passing had been illuminated occasionally by flashes from Mam's Good Luck star, being released from the deadening influence of Mr Alkman's regime, and finding senior school to my liking. But the Bad Luck star which had guided the tipsy midwife to my birth in Hollis Street struck again. My right foot – the one which the midwife had twisted, was hurting a lot. A visit with Mam to a bleak consulting room in the General Hospital confirmed our own doctor's diagnosis that I would have to undergo an operation if I wasn't going to be crippled by the deformed foot. I thought of Ernie's dad and the ugly built-up boot he had to wear. The fear-induced image of myself in such a monstrosity appalled me so much that I was impatient to be called by the surgeon to Harlow Wood, an orthopaedic hospital near Mansfield.

There would be some compensations for a few weeks in hospital: there would be no more queuing at the Co-op; no more reluctant errands to the bookie's back door, and I would be out of earshot of Mam's never-ending complaints about her penury. There might be pain involved, but I had got used to that, and the thought of lying in bed with all the time in the world to read was a promise of rosy days to come.

Chapter 16

The Prize Rabbit

I rarely saw Alan now, but guessed his claustrophobic life continued within the same miserly boundaries imposed by his stepmother, and perhaps by his own reluctance to make friends of those of us who liked to roam the streets and fields. We chatted briefly if we met on our journeys to and from school, but the memory of my bullying him always acted as a constraint between us.

One Saturday night the bullying took on a crueller form when Ernie and I invaded the house – the inner sanctum itself. On one of his solitary night sorties through the neighbourhood back gardens in the blackout, Ernie had discovered a rabbit cage which stood next to the Carey back door. It housed a beautiful white rabbit with a black butterfly pattern on its muzzle. This made the animal a special one for Ernie. He believed that the butterfly marking on a rabbit's nose made it special, indicated that it was a prize rodent. Ernie wanted it so much he was even prepared to buy it if the Careys were willing to sell. Although I was uneasy about going to the house, Ernie's presence was reassuring. After all, I told myself, it was a legitimate visit, and Ernie would be doing all the talking. He had no qualms about the visit: he knew little about Alan, and nothing about the smothering vigilance of Mrs Carey because I'd never talked to him about it. I kept quiet about my surprise that the Carey's had been soft-hearted enough to buy Alan a pet rabbit.

When we went round to the back door, Ernie leading the way confidently, we could see the rabbit poking its nose through the chicken-wire of its cage. It was a fine looking buck in prime condition, and I could see why Ernie coveted it. As he knocked loudly on the door I winced, knowing that Mrs Carey would not be impressed by his boldness. But it was Alan who opened the door, his thin nose poking through the narrow gap he allowed himself. He was plainly worried by our presence, his bony face taking on the haunted look I knew so well.

"What d'you want?" he asked nervously. His chest wheezed as though he had a touch of bronchitis.

"How much do you want for your rabbit?" Ernie demanded.

"It's not for sale," Alan replied sullenly. "It's my dad's – he's not selling it." He closed the door on us, but Ernie pushed it open again.

"Hang on!" Ernie forced the door open wider with his shoulder. I didn't like the way things were developing. I waited for Mrs Carey to appear in that spooky way she had. If she showed, I was going to run for it. "I'll give you a couple of bob for it," Ernie persisted.

Alan had his shoulder behind the door, trying to prevent Ernie pushing it open wider. "I've told you – it's not for sale, it belongs to my dad. It's a prize rabbit. Get off the door, please. I've got to shut it." He was close to tears. Ernie was looking at the rabbit as it gazed over the neat rows of vegetables in the garden.

"Ask your dad how much he wants for it. We'll wait here."

"My dad isn't in. He's gone to the pictures with our mam. Will you please go now – I'll get into trouble if they find out I've opened the door!"

This was Alan's biggest mistake, and Ernie picked it up straight away. "Can we come in for a bit then?" It was a signal of intent rather than a request. It was the normal thing to do. You were always allowed into a pal's house if his mam and dad were out. It was a good chance to poke around to see how well off they were in comparison to your own family. The most obvious way was to examine the furniture and the knick-knacks they possessed. Ernie had told me that the best way to tell if people were well off was to listen for echoes when you knocked at the door, or if somebody walked about the house. Echoes meant that there wasn't much furniture upstairs – perhaps only the beds. A hollow sound from the bedrooms was a sure sign of poverty. That was how he found out that our house was poor, he informed me.

Alan looked towards me, as if for succour. But Ernie in this mood was implacable. Besides, I was eager to see the Carey shrine for the first time. Alan's face was white with stress. "Our dad'll kill me if I let anybody in. Please go now!"

Ernie put his shoulder to the door and suddenly we were in the kitchen. "You got any lemonade?" he asked, quite politely. He was opening and closing cupboard doors and drawers, inspecting their contents.

"You rotten buggers!" Alan wailed. Tears were running down his face. "I'm telling our mam when she comes home. She'll have the police on you!"

"Don't be so mardy," Ernie said, and strolled into the living-room with Alan dancing in distress at his heels.

I followed, but I was nervous. I knew that I would have to pay for this escapade. I watched Ernie potter about the comfortably furnished, immaculate room. No echoes here. He lifted lids, opened drawers, sifted through their contents. I hung back, scared, yet maliciously enjoying the comic suffering of Alan. He was wringing his hands as if he was soaping them. He danced from one foot to the other like little kids do when they're dying to go for a pee.

Ernie pulled out a bundle of letters from a drawer. "Don't touch them!" Alan pleaded. "They're from my dad. He has to work away sometimes, building things for the army." Ernie took one of the letters out of its envelope. I could see it began *My dearest darling* ... Alan snatched it out of his hand. Ernie laughed, taking a final look around the room. "Nice house," he said. "You must be well off."

"Mind your own business!" Alan said, and I was suddenly scared that he was different somehow, a look of defiance in his eyes. He stood in front of the sideboard as if he was prepared to fight to protect its contents. I just hoped that Ernie didn't hit him – we were in enough trouble as it was. But Ernie shrugged. "Let's go," he said, as if he was bored by Alan and his house, then walked out.

Left alone with Alan I felt ashamed that I had allowed him to be put through such an ordeal when I could easily have stopped it. "We didn't do anything," I said, weak and embarrassed.

Alan's eyes were full of hate. "I'm going to tell on you. You've got me into trouble, but you're in trouble as well. You know what our mam's like. She'll blame me for letting you in."

"Sorry," I mumbled. "I'll see you at school, then?"

"Bogger off, you bastard!" Alan said, and he was close to tears again.

I caught up with Ernie as he swaggered down Bradfield Road, whistling, his hands thrust into his trouser pockets. I was too full of my own shame and apprehension to talk to him.

Alan carried out his threat to tell his stepmother about our invasion of their home. Mrs Carey sent Alan across to summon Mam to listen to her tale of woe about me. That was bad enough, but Mrs Carey also complained that some special coins were missing. I don't know what made them special, but their disappearance turned a stupid escapade into a criminal act. I guessed that Ernie might have taken them when he rummaged through the drawers, although I hadn't noticed him secrete them. I did remember that he had his hands in his pockets as we walked away, and that was unusual for Ernie. He might have been grasping those rotten coins. It dawned on me that Alan might have craftily taken them to heat up the accusations against me. If he had, it was a pretty smart thing to do, and worthy of using in a story for Mr Sadler in English.

I managed to convince both Mam and Mrs Carey of my innocence in the case of the missing coins. Mam always knew when I was lying, and she convinced the affronted Mrs Carey that I really didn't know about the coins, though there would be a pasting due for the uninvited entry into the house. I had to promise that I would never go near the house again, and that I would leave Alan alone. It was a promise that I had made myself, anyway.

I decided to keep away from Ernie, too, for a while. Life was much simpler without him. But a few days later I was crossing the wasteground, which lay between his back garden and the shops, when I glanced across at his house. There on the path under the kitchen window was a rabbit cage, and in the cage sat a white rabbit with a black butterfly pattern on its nose. I flew round to the house.

"You've nicked Carey's rabbit!" I choked. "I'm in enough trouble there as it is! It's stupid! Everybody can see it from the wasteground."

"It ent Carey's rabbit," Ernie said, infuriatingly calm. "I got it from the cattle market on Wednesday. It's called Blacky."

"It's pissing white," I protested, knowing he had thought the name up that very second. "It's Carey's rabbit! It's got the butterfly on its nose!"

"There's millions of rabbits with a butterfly on their noses. They're nothing special. The bloke down the cattle market told me. You can get one for a shilling."

"That's Carey's rabbit," I insisted. "And I'm going to take it back. I'll just tell them I found it hopping about on Bradfield Road."

"No you're not," Ernie said with a hint of threat. "I'll tek it back tomorrow. I'll tell our dad it's died." He poked his finger into the cage to make the rabbit move. "Rabbits are boring, anyway. Our old man's gonna buy me a dog next time we go to the cattle market. An alsation."

I felt the theft of the rabbit as a betrayal, and I wondered why I stuck with Ernie. But I knew the answer already: the past few days without him had been deadly dull.

The next time I saw Alan he asked me if I knew anything about their rabbit, which had been stolen. I pleaded my innocence, but wondered why Ernie hadn't taken it back. Perhaps he daren't risk it. After all, a story about finding a rabbit hopping about on Bradfield Road didn't sound so plausible now. Mrs Carey would never believe it. I no longer cared whether Alan believed in my innocence or not. He was a lost cause. But the Careys never did see their rabbit again. When I went to call on Ernie his rabbit cage had gone, and so had the rabbit. I felt a bit sick when he told me what had happened to it. "After all," he said, "you eat owt when there's a war on."

*   *   *

Sometimes I retreated from Ernie's dubious friendship. But I always sought him out, eventually, when other consolations such as reading, day-dreaming or just walking failed. We both joined the gang of kids absorbed by the harmless games of the street, climbed the spiked railings of the green in front of Mo's house to make up play or joined the meandering conversations that were about nothing, and went nowhere except to laughter. We had a sense of being in a world of our own making, untouched by grim-faced adults on the other side of the spikes. And perhaps *they* were suspicious of our sudden silence if they came near, remembering from their own childhood, if they had the imagination, that there is a part of it which cannot be touched by adults, that is secret, and cruel.

Chapter 17

Harlow Wood

The weeks of waiting to go into hospital drifted into months. My initial impatience to get the operation on my foot over and done with faded into indifference. I all but forgot what lay in store for me. When the summons to the hospital finally slipped through the letterbox I was excited, at first, although the excitement changed to fear when I recalled an earlier operation on my foot. The memory was hazy, almost dreamlike, but I saw figures in white gowns and masks moving under bright lights. I remembered, too, the smell of ether and the frightening feeling of disembodiment as I sank into unconsciousness. I was seven years old when I had that first operation on my foot, and remembered how much going under the anaesthetic had scared me. I didn't tell Mam that I was afraid. Gradually, the fear subsided. I was twelve years old now, not seven. I consoled myself with the thought that the ordeal would be worth going through if the reward was to be a "normal" foot.

Harlow Wood Orthopaedic Hospital was situated fifteen miles from Nottingham in an undulating landscape of plantations, woods and fields. Gazing out of the window of the bus on my way there. Mam by my side, I was fascinated by the neat arrangement of the countryside. It seemed so ordered, so well kept it could have been the work of gardeners rather than of farmers. Perhaps it was the light covering of snow under which it lay that gave the impression of tidiness. Under a snow-filled sky the horizon was hard to distinguish, giving the whole scene a sense of enormous distances.

As Mam and I trudged up the long drive through fir trees I got my first glimpse of the hospital. It looked like a school campus with its clusters of single-storey wooden buildings separated by patches of open ground. Its homely appearance helped to settle the butterflies in my stomach as we approached the entrance, with Mam carrying my borrowed suitcase.

We were led into a dressing-room where an admissions nurse instructed me to get undressed. I obeyed self-consciously, quickly hiding my naked body in the new pyjamas that smelled of Staddon's store, and were specially bought for the occasion. I said a brief good-bye to Mam, hardly aware of her in my nervousness, then climbed into the high, beautifully soft and comfortable hospital bed that was mine for a few weeks. I caught a final glimpse of Mam as she hurried down the long, snow covered drive. I wanted her to turn and wave at me, but she walked with her head down as if she was absorbed, her hands thrust deep in the pockets of her shabby coat, until she disappeared among the fir trees.

I was wheeled out of the dressing-room and into a hut-like ward that housed about twenty boy patients. Those either side of my bed gave me no more than a cursory glance, a show of indifference which seemed unfriendly. Later, I learned that they had been in the ward for a long time, the helpless witnesses of many arrivals, and mine was nothing special. I was immediately homesick. I thought of Mam sitting alone on the bus as she made the long journey back to Broxtowe, an image which brought embarrassing tears to my eyes. The dark-haired, pale-faced boy in the next bed propped himself on his elbow, turned his head stiffly to talk to me.

"What're you in for?" he asked.

"An operation on my foot."

"Just your foot?"

I was piqued by the dismissive tone of his question. Having surgeons cutting into my foot seemed pretty serious to me.

"I've had seven operations," he informed me, totally matter-of-fact. "I'm having another one soon." He rolled down his bed-sheets to reveal a trunk and legs completely encased in plaster. I was shocked.

"What's wrong with you?" I asked.

"T.B. hip. Most of us have got T.B. hip or spine. T.B. spine is worst. One lad's had about twelve operations. He was scalded, though. He has skin grafts."

"How long have you been here?" I couldn't drag my eyes from the repulsive, hard white case he was trapped in.

"Over two years. Some've been here longer. How long you in for?"

"Five weeks," I said. It seemed a pathetically short period, now. On the bus journey here it had seemed like an eternity.

The boy smiled, but it was as bleak as the winter landscape outside. "That's just a weekend," he said, then lay back to stare out of the French-windows which formed one side of the ward.

I settled into the routine of the hospital, feeling that I was lucky not to be as ill as the rest of the boys. My fear eased when I learned that mine was to be a "minor" operation. I became confident enough to ask a nurse what, exactly, the surgeon was going to do to my foot. She laughed. "Don't worry," she said. "You won't feel a thing." The quiet, withdrawn boy in the next bed had been justified, perhaps, in his dismissal of my slight deformity. He didn't know when he would go home, although he was being treated with a new "miracle" drug called penicillin. It had already speeded his recovery, providing him with new hope that one day he would return to his home in Gainsborough.

I managed to satisfy my curiosity about the surgeon's plan for my foot when he talked to the young men in white coats who trailed after him as he made his rounds in the ward. Eavesdropping was the only way to learn what adults were plotting in their more interesting conversations – those not destined for children's ears. The surgeon would break a bone in my foot, he told his acolytes the day before my operation. Then he would re-set it. Half of my little toe would be amputated, which was plain enough, although the rest was a bit confusing: he would do something with a tendon or muscle – I thought I heard him use the word "transplant", but I couldn't be sure. When the nodding group of white-coats moved on I tried to clarify the point with a nurse. "Are they going to transplant my muscle?" I enquire politely. The nurse stifled a laugh, then called her companion over. She told me to ask the question again. Both nurses giggled when I repeated it. I couldn't understand why, and felt foolish.

"It'll be something like that," one of the nurses said. "Don't worry about it. You'll be fine. We'll look after you."

"Will you be here when I wake up?"

"It depends how long you sleep. We'll see you some time tomorrow, anyway. Now I've got to shave your leg."

Both nurses were young and teasingly good natured. They made me feel safe, their laughter putting me at ease as they prepared me for surgery. As a porter pushed me on a trolley along the corridor to the operating theatre, the nurse held my hand. Someone put a mask over my face. A voice asked me to count to ten, then I slipped into darkness.

I regained consciousness feeling nauseous. But my favourite nurse was there, slapping my wrists, her soothing voice close to my ear. I felt strange, everything was on a different plane. I was only half-way back to myself. "Do you want to see your pot leg?" the nurse smiled.

There it was: pristine white, covering my foot and my leg up to my knee, but open at the toes.

"You've done well," the nurse said. "Most boys cry when they come round."

I was too tired to cry, too far away. All I wanted to do was sleep.

* * *

I woke to excruciating pain. My foot was being crushed in a vice that closed with unrelenting power on my toes. I called out in the semi-darkness of the deserted dressing-room. It must have come out as a yell because a nurse came running from the ward. Consoling words, a sip of water, my pillows shaken into softness – none of it drove the pain away. The dim night-light illuminated glass cabinets containing bottles and jars, silver instruments and red, coiled lengths of rubber tubing. Each object seemed endowed with the power to inflict pain. I had felt pain before, but not like this.

A doctor arrived, his hair dishevelled as though he had just crawled out of bed. He spoke to the nurse and she gave me a tablet to swallow, the water cooling my parched throat. Gradually, drowsiness pulled me out of the vice and into a painless darkness again.

I came round to the sound of the surgeon's voice, and it was morning. The pain had subsided into a throbbing ache. The surgeon was demonstrating something to a younger man using his hands, indicating a shape. It was as though he was using sign language. I couldn't connect his surreal performance with myself until the fog inside my head had cleared a little. There was a sharpness in his voice that conveyed anger, the serious look on the face of the younger man suggesting that he was being reprimanded. Something had gone wrong, a mistake had been made. That much I could tell. The bungling midwife was reaching out across twelve years to harm me again. After the surgery, it appeared, the young doctor had been given the task of applying the plaster bandages to my foot. Disastrously, he had pressed the foot back into its original deformed shape. When the plaster dried my foot was forced out of its new configuration by the vice-like grip of the cast. The plaster would have to be cut off, and a new cast applied.

I was pushed to a part of the hospital I hadn't seen before: a bright, white tiled room that reflected the hard glare of the winter sun and seemed like an extension of the snowy landscape outside. A young man in a white coat picked up a pair of long-handled cutters and I flinched. "Nothing to worry about," he smiled. "I promise I won't cut your leg off," and he laughed. "Just lie back and relax." The cutters crunched through the plaster. I felt nothing, for the young man took great care, winking at me when he saw me watching his handiwork. "Nearly done," he said. I watched with growing interest as he soaked broad bandages in a bowl of creamy plaster before winding them gently around my foot and leg. Even the ache had gone with the removal of the cast. I lay back, now, as he wound the comforting wet strips, to examine the plaster models of feet and legs on the walls. They were representations of twisted toes, arches and ankles – all of them contorted deformities, a nightmare collection which scared me. They were set out on shelves as though the room was a museum, a chamber of horrors that Ernie, Mo and the rest of the Withern Road gang would have paid to see.

In the late afternoon my bed was steered back to the ward. The long night had taken on the unreality of a half-remembered dream. I was hungry now. It seemed like days since I had last eaten. Now all I had to do, I thought, was to lie back to wait out the four weeks left to me. Then I would be able to tell my pals about the plaster-cast museum and the lads in body-casts, the young doctor's bungling of my cast application and giant pair of cutters that looked capable of slicing a leg off. Soon it would be supper time. With luck it would be shepherd's pie and bread pudding, a satisfying feast of stodge that I relished. Now that the worst part of my ordeal was over, I could become a genuine, bed-ridden patient, anchored as I was by my new pot leg. The cast wasn't completely dry yet. A wire cage under the sheets held them off my leg while their ends were folded back so that my feet were exposed to the air. That fact was something I overlooked, later, when I agreed to spend the night out on the wintry verandah.

Although most of the boys in the ward were immobilized by their body casts, one or two of the more adventurous used a technique of propelling their beds so that they could visit each other when the nurses were busy elsewhere. This involved what they called "paddling": It required a rubber-tipped walking stick which was used as a paddle to drive the bed forward and backward. A hard push on the floor with the paddle would set the bed into squeaky, lumbering motion up and down the ward like an ungainly canoe. The game went on until a nurse caught a "paddler" in mid-ward. The nurse would push the bed back into its place with a mock-serious warning that all walking-sticks would be taken away if there was anymore wandering beds.

I was encouraged to try "paddling" with my own new walking-stick by Ken, a burly, cheerful lad from Nottingham whose T.B. hip made him a long-stay patient. It looked like fun, and a few days after my return to the ward I was steering my bed up and down the aisle as though I was canoeing on the Trent. One day, in the hiatus between tea and supper when the nurses left us alone, Ken shouted across to me. "D'you fancy sleeping out tonight?" He explained that some nights he and one or two other "paddlers" opened the French-windows with their walking sticks, then manoeuvred their beds onto the open verandah which overlooked miles of fields and woods rolling away towards Mansfield. "It's great!" he enthused. "We come back in before the day nurses come on duty. Sometimes the night nurses find us and push us back. But mostly we get away with it. Come on – it's just like camping!"

I didn't take much persuading, mainly because Ken's approach was an offer of friendship I was happy to accept. I was uneasy about the cold-looking landscape, wondering how bitter it might be at night. The beautiful fir trees with their decorative dusting of snow provided a picture attractive enough for a christmas card, but it was best observed from indoors rather than from such close quarters as the verandah. I kept my reservations to myself, though, in case Ken thought me weak.

When the lights went out that evening we feigned sleep for a few minutes, then made our move. With the ease of an expert Ken lifted the bolt on the French-window with his walking-stick, then pushed it open. I shivered as cold air rushed into the ward. Ken paddled his bed onto the verandah and I followed, pushing the French-window to with my stick. The boy from Gainsborough, who had refused to come out with us, struggled with his stick to push the bolt back. I snuggled into my pillow to gaze up into a sky of spiralling light and frost-sharp stars. There was a piercing yelp from the darkness of the fields which startled me. It sounded like some beast out of a Boris Karloff horror film. "A fox," Ken explained. "There's dozens of them round here." The cold penetrated my sheets and chilled my body, but I didn't want to go back inside. Ken and I might have been the only people awake in the world, so tangible was the silence after the fox's call. How long we lay talking in a whisper, or just stared up at the sky's effulgence, I don't know. When Ken no longer responded to my whispers I was lulled into sleep, so cold now that I seemed to be at one with the freezing woods and the foxes.

When I woke in the first dull grey light of morning I was in pain again. I whispered hoarsely to Ken, and he stirred. "I'm freezing!" he complained, his teeth chattering as if to confirm it. "Wake somebody up."

I tapped lightly on the French-window with my walking-stick, my fingers so cold I could hardly grasp it. I saw the thin white arm of the boy from Gainsborough reach out as he manipulated the bolt with the crook of his stick. He slid the bolt and pushed the French-window open. Stiffly, Ken and I paddled back to our places in the ward. The toes on my plastered foot were burning, then went numb.

When the day nurse strolled into the ward to wake the boys, Ken was shivering uncontrollably. She hurried to him, felt his hands, his face, put the end of his sheet to her face. I could hear her angry voice, but couldn't make out what she was saying. Ken must have revealed our secret. She came across to me, felt my hands, face and sheets. "You idiots!" she snapped. "You could have frozen to death. I wouldn't be in your shoes when the doctor finds out!"

I hadn't seen my shoes for some time, but the unconscious irony of her threat didn't seem funny at that moment.

"Let's get these sheets changed," she fussed.

I was worried about the deadness in my toes, but I was reluctant to mention it in case it brought more of her wrath upon my head. It was only when my sheets had been changed, and her good humour returned, that I expressed my anxiety.

"I think there's something wrong with my toes," I confessed meekly.

"Are they hurting?"

"No. I can't feel them."

A worried look clouded her face. She pinched one of my toes. "Can you feel that?"

"No."

She pinched another toe. "How about that?"

"I can't feel anything. It's sort of numb."

My bed was pushed into the dressing-room, and a doctor fetched.

"You spent the night outside, I hear," he drawled laconically as he squeezed the toes inside my cast. I couldn't feel his fingers. "That wasn't very bright, was it? Can you feel that?"

"No," I said in answer to both questions, my voice small with embarrassment.

"It was a very silly thing to do, wasn't it?"

I nodded, dumb with remorse and shame. The doctor took a needle of the nurse's dish and pricked it into my toes. I flinched at the action, but felt nothing. He might have been sticking the needle into his own toe for all the sensation I felt. "Can you feel anything? The slightest tingle?"

I shook my head.

"It's frostbite," he drawled with surgical calm. He was talking to the nurse, but I think he wanted to frighten me, rather than inform her of what she probably knew, anyway.

I spent the rest of the day in the isolation of the dressing-room, a hot-water bottle clamped over the gap in my cast to thaw my frozen toes. There were regular examinations by the nurse, her annoyance subsiding with every visit to jab a needle into a toe to test for feeling. Towards evening my favourite nurse, the breezy girl who had prepared me for the operation, arrived to have her turn with the needle. "You silly boy!" she mocked. "And here was I thinking you looked intelligent. It just shows how wrong you can be. I don't know. What are we going to do with you? Perhaps I should ask the doctor to transplant your brains!"

Her mischievous reference to my question made me feel better. Surely she wouldn't tease me if I was in serious danger. Later that evening she thrust the needle in and I yelled in shock as I felt pain at last. "That's better," she grinned. "Now we won't have to chop your big toe off!" She must have noticed how much the thought of it worried me. "Don't worry," she said. "I was only joking!"

Fortunately, there was no lasting damage to complicate the surgeon's work so I was wheeled back into the ward in time for supper. Ken was smirking at my return. He had escaped with no more than a telling-off and a change of sheets. I resolved that my first expedition outside would also be my last. It was time to slip quietly into the routine life of the ward if I wasn't to be regarded as a nuisance by the good-natured nurses.

I had my discharge to look forward to in a matter of weeks. Most of the other boys could not see the end of their treatment. They were confined within the rectangle of the cream painted ward, their space limited to an area taken up by a bed and a cupboard stuffed with personal possessions. Time was measured by meal times, the day divided by changes to dressings – some of which smelled foul – the call for urine bottles and bedpans. The only excitement was provided by visiting hours on Saturdays and Sundays. No visitor ever came during the week. Some families travelled long distances bearing gifts of fruit, comics and bottles of barley water or orange squash. Occasionally, an anxious parent would be led into the office to receive reports from a doctor of the success, or otherwise, of treatment. Reports were given, also, on operations recently carried out. News of forthcoming operations was also conveyed to parents. They would return with the secret of the consultation locked behind a forced smile. The news of an impending operation sometimes brought joy, for it was a step forward in recovery, a positive act in a life of passive waiting.

The slowness of the hours was a subtle torture to me. I longed to expend the energy which was natural to me. I wasn't *really* ill – I just had a pot leg, that's all! It was hard to distinguish one day from another, so uniform were they. A trolley loaded with books of the educational and uplifting kind was pushed from bed to bed once a week. I ignored dull tomes with titles like *50 Things To Do With Paper And Scissors*, *A Missionary In China*, or *Great Inventions Of The Twentieth Century*, searching through the collection for adventure novels. In the mornings we were given half-hearted lessons in arithmetic, English and handicraft that no-one could be bothered with. Some boys were too ill to bother, others too bored. I learned a little about leatherwork, but preferred to read a novel or write long, rambling letters to Mam, none of which she ever saw because they were too emotional. They conveyed a homesickness and affection that it would have been impossible to speak of, and would have embarrassed her. As a family, we just didn't express such sentiment. I wouldn't have been able to face her on her next visit if I had been so open as to send her one of my confessions of filial love.

I was conscious, always, of my luck in being such a minor patient. The T.B. hips and spines of the other boys denied them the robust independence of my own life, and that of my pals. Never, for these boys, would there be the freedom and devilment of street games, the pleasures of tree-climbing and garden-hopping, the casual danger of scrumping. They were missing the absorbing trivia of meandering talk as they sat on the edge of a gutter or wandered across forbidden fields. It seemed to me that bad luck had denied Ken and the boy from Gainsborough life itself. Shackled by body casts, they were being cheated. Some of the other boys rarely spoke, their enforced isolation making them passive, and painfully shy.

At last, I was taken down to the chamber of horrors again, this time to have an iron hoop moulded onto my cast so that I could walk. When it had dried, I took my first wobbling steps with the aid of my walking stick, and a nurse. Soon I was limping up and down the ward. I discovered boys at the top end that I had never noticed before. One thin, old-looking boy, about ten years of age, lay in a cast from his neck to his toes. He told me, without a trace of self-pity, that he had been in Harlow Wood for three years. He had forgotten how many operations had been carried out on his spine, knowing only that he was due for another quite soon, and that it didn't bother him any more.

I desperately wanted to get out then, frightened by what he had to bear, and awed by his acceptance of it. I was shamed, too, by my cowardice in not being able to walk as far as his bed again, even though he had asked me to.

I had expected Mam to collect me from the hospital, and a ride home in an ambulance. Instead, I was driven home by a smartly dressed, well-spoken man, a hospital volunteer. He was rather posh, but friendly as we chattered in his luxurious Daimler. He delivered me to our front door complete with my walking-stick and my shabby suitcase containing my pyjamas, toothbrush, one shoe, and a leather purse I had made for Mam in the hospital's handicraft sessions.

The living-room had shrunk to the size of a cupboard, the furniture was rougher than I remembered it, and the room was cold after the constant, even warmth of the ward. But Mam was waiting, and she was smiling. On the table set for dinner was this week's *Dandy*. I was home.

Chapter 18

Soldiers

My leg began to itch after a few weeks inside its plaster cast. Down went a pencil, a knitting-needle, a ruler – any implement which could reach the prickling torment around my ankle. I went limping up to Strelley village, crashed through waist-high weeds in the woods, laying a path for Ernie and Mo. I kept goal in games of football on Withern Road green, although I could only leap to my left. I bored holes in the soft asphalt of the pavement by spinning on my iron hoop to make chocks for games of marbles. The white cast became soiled with mud, tar, grass stains and the gang's autographs. Frays and gashes appeared where the cast had been snagged on the spiked railings which we had to climb over to reach our football pitch. The only thing I couldn't do was to climb trees.

I wallowed in my freedom like a newly released convict, ignoring Mam's warnings to "take care". That was for cripples, and I was determined that I wouldn't be one. But I had too much time to myself. I resented being kept off school. After all, I reasoned, if I could play football, I could sit quietly behind a desk. A doctor at the General Hospital refused to allow it, then told me off for the battered state of my cast.

The days dragged, as they had in Harlow Wood, after a couple of weeks at home. Yet there were compensations. I stumped down to the Aspley library, read my way through the day until Ernie and Mo returned from school. Some days I spent at Aunt Edie's listening to her radio, conscious that such luxury was sanctioned by authority. Best of all were the afternoons when I had managed to scrape ninepence together for a show at the almost deserted Forum. I sat with old-age pensioners, the daft and the skivers in the stale aroma of the previous night's cigarettes, losing myself in the screen's fiction. It seemed like a wicked act to be the only school-kid in the place, gazing up at the art-deco glitter of a Hollywood musical to watch Alice Faye or Betty Grable moon through their love songs, the noise of a number 16 bus chugging up Aspley Lane filtering into the auditorium. In between buses I was lost in my trance, and only a hint of sunlight flashing in the darkness at the back when a pensioner went out for a pee reminded me that it was mid-afternoon, and that the rest of the world had its head bowed under the whip of work, study and duty.

I was kept at home for three months before the cast was cut off at the General Hospital, revealing my wasted leg and a straightened foot, marred now by a long, thin scar like a fishbone. There were weekly sessions of physiotherapy to attend at the Cripples Guild, but people no longer stared at me as they did when I limped along with my pot leg.

I returned for the final term of my second year in the senior school with few regrets for my lost leisure. I worked with an enthusiasm that seemed to take the teachers by surprise, eager to catch up on lost lessons, determined to appear as "normal" as possible. Before the school broke up for the long summer holiday I had managed to win the "progress prize", as well as prizes in English, history and geography. But Mam read my glowing report without enthusiasm, even though I had come first in half of the subjects. "You'll be better off earning a wage," she sniffed. "It's time I had some help off somebody." Already she was looking forward to the day, only six months ahead, when I would be 14, the school leaving age, and ready for work. I would spend only one term in my third year before my education finished, leaving at the christmas break, a week before my 14th birthday. I tried to persuade Mam to let me stay on at school for the whole year – I would still be only 14 years old, but she was determined to see me out at work and earning by then.

On prize-giving night I took the stage in the school hall as Quince in *A Midsummer Night's Dream*, a production we had rehearsed for weeks. It must have been a very truncated version of the play as it lasted less than an hour, concentrating on the fairies and the artisans, sugar-paper spectacle and belly-laughs. The year's smallest lad was Puck, and Titania was a skinny effeminate with a high-pitched voice, forever after known as "Tit". My gang of artisans were chosen for their reading ability rather than for their acting talent, as I probably was, too. Bottom was selected because he was the only fat lad in the year, that being considered comical enough. Mr Smith, our English and music teacher, used his record of Mendelssohn's incidental music, and that gave the production a touch of class, we thought. None of us really understood what the play was about, or even liked it very much, and the polite applause at the end of its only performance was probably for our nerve rather than out talent.

It was a busy, exciting evening for me, and Mam was there to witness it – as far as I remember, the only time she ever came to the school. Apart from appearing in the play, I had to collect my progress prize, then joined the school choir. We sang a few sea shanties because such songs allowed a bit of roughness in the voices, and we had plenty of that. But I felt ridiculous when we had to imitate the action of hauling in ropes or climbing up rigging as we sang *Blow The Man Down*, and I wondered what Mam was thinking, and if it made her more determined to see me doing something useful and wage-earning in a factory. I walked home with Mam at the end of it all. I was full of myself, my head swimming with success, the prize book clutched to my chest so that everyone could see I was a winner. "Did you like the play?" I asked tentatively.

"You played your part well enough," she answered, her eyes still glazed with apparent boredom. "I didn't understand the story though. What was it supposed to be about?" She must have detected my dejection at her cold-water response. "I felt proud when you went up for your prize," she said in consolation. "And the choir sang nice."

* * *

My new mobility meant that I could be in Strelley village after a few minutes' walk. When I was alone I always crept into the weathered sandstone church to marvel at its eerie silence, breathe in the age-evoking scent of old polish and dust. The creamy alabaster effigy of a de Strelley knight reposed peacefully in the gloom. I knew of no other place which harboured such quiet. The faintest creak of a pew or the heavy porch door was a whisper from the middle ages, the worn slabs of the floor holding in the past buried beneath my feet. I imagined the bones of dead generations lying there, projected my own fancy into the place and it became mysterious, sometimes a little frightening, every sound, even that of the draught under the door, becoming a voice telling its story. Compared to this ancient, awesome place, Broxtowe estate lay at the dog-end of time, a place without a history. A mile away stood the row of shops with its queues of patient, shuffling women clutching their ration books, complaining about points and coupons, the shortages of food, and the difficulties of making meals. Buses pulled away from the terminus on Beechdale Road to begin the journey to town. Old men waited outside the Beacon for opening time, reading the *Racing Tissue*. What had that to do with the romantic past of chivalry and knights, I wondered. How did we get from the Norman knights of Strelley to the mean-souled Mr Alkman and the schoolboard man? I tried to imagine what the de Strelley world might have been like, and where our family would have fitted in the scheme of things. I had no doubt we would have been in lowly occupations, although I might have been picked out to be trained as a squire to a crusading de Strelley. My picture of that world was composed partly of facts elicited from the text book at school, but mainly from seeing Errol Flynn in *Robin Hood* at the Forum.

The countryside had its attractions and its mysteries. But it was the act of walking itself which became an obsession as I fought against the fear of being lame. I defied the ache which gripped me after I had walked a mile. I was trying to develop the muscles in my slightly withered leg, thinking that every ache meant further development, and more strength. Images of the boys in Harlow Wood stretched out in the prisons of their plaster casts drove me to walk beyond caring about the pain. The memory of Ken, and of the boy I saw only once at the top of the ward, drove me on. As the months passed, I was able to walk longer distances before the ache began. Then there was no ache at all.

Part of my self-imposed recuperative routine was to take regular three-mile walks on Sunday mornings to visit my Buttress grandparents in New Basford. Over the months, the visits developed their own ritual. On entering the tiny living room I waited by the ornament-cluttered sideboard until I was invited to sit down on the prickly horse-hair chaiselongue close to the black-leaded fireplace. I was offered a drink after my long walk, usually water, but sometimes, as a treat, Grandma brought in a cup of cabbage water from the kitchen. She had great faith in it as an antidote to acne, visible or potential, and as a potion promoting general good health – a kind of folk medicine. After I had answered the routine questions about the health of Mam, Brenda and the "young 'un" whose name they could never remember, I was invited to read the latest issue of *John Bull* magazine which was neatly stashed with copies of the week's *Evening Post* under the cushions of the chaiselongue. I was conscious, always, of the difference between Mam's easy going, rough-tongued family and the polite restraint of the Buttress clan. I was never sure where I belonged. Mam would accuse me of being too much of a "Buttress" if I was acting leary. Aunt Mabel supported her in this. "You're just like your Dad!" was the worst insult she used when she thought I had behaved badly in some way. Although I always felt more at ease with my Radford aunts and cousins, the Buttress house on Hollis Street held pleasant memories of my early childhood, and was special because it was the house in which I had been born. It also provided a respite from the tensions of home. The glass case over the piano displaying Grandad's Great War medals, badges, and a bullet taken from his leg, the dull "tock" of the pendulum wall-clock, the photographs of Dad's handsome sisters, the neat, shining brass furnished hearth – all evoked memories of a time I had felt secure, happy, looked after by relatives who were kinder towards me than they sometimes were to each other.

My visits were less formal, more enjoyable if my youthful aunts, Dorothy and Violet were at home. Both were young women now. Violet was very pretty, like her older sisters, though volatile and possessed a cutting, sarcastic tongue. This defect was balanced by a mischievous sense of humour and a talent for wicked mimicry with which she entertained me. She was also generous now she was working for a living. I was always sent on my way with a piece of silver in my pocket. She argued remorselessly with Dorothy, who was too placid and soft-hearted to be a match for her younger sister. I loved both of them, for they were just as concerned for me as they had been when they had acted like caring older sisters in the years just before the war began.

Grandad had a reticence that Dad had inherited. But he was warm towards me, making an effort at conversation that was always friendly and encouraging. I sensed he was making a real effort, one that I appreciated. The affection he displayed helped to compensate for the lack of it from Dad. A disciplinarian with his own children, he was relaxed and good humoured with me. As he grew older, he was less able to impose his rigid, old-fashioned notions of male authority on his self-assured daughters. Dad, on leave and in uniform, was still humble in the presence of the old man. Only the younger son, Arthur, handsome and silver-tongued, the black sheep of the family because of his womanizing and infidelity, was like his sisters in self-possession and confidence. He had the audacity to laugh at the old man's attempts to bully him. Arthur had been thrown down the stairs and out of the house when he was eighteen years old. Left to fend for himself, he had made his way in the world as a civil engineer, and he wasn't going to allow an ageing Edwardian to cramp his amoral zest for wine, women and song.

When Grandad stood up from his chair by the hearth to comb his hair, fine textured and still fair, it was twelve o'clock, time for his weekly stroll down to the Royal Oak for his game of dominoes, and time for me to make the journey home to Broxtowe, two bus rides away. The following week the ritual would be played out again like some restrained celebration of the family with its own symbolic acts of welcome and hospitality, its litany of kindly intended questions and advice that seemed to acknowledge that I lived with unhappy parents.

* * *

I crossed the boundary between my brief past and my present when I visited my grandparents. I learned to see how a few years could change the world around me, and change me. One of the external changes I became aware of was the mood of people as the war dragged on into its fourth year. The weary acceptance of rationing and restriction, the growing shabbiness of the fabric of our lives, was eased at last by an optimism that perhaps the end of war was something it was possible to visualize. The rumours of a "second front", the invasion of France which would finally defeat Hitler was made manifest by the arrival of the Yanks, paratroopers, who set up camp in the beautiful grounds of Wollaton Hall on the edge of the city. The ornate Elizabethan building looked down from its hill onto landscaped trees, a lake and sweeping green acres over which roamed a herd of deer the Yanks took pot-shots at with their rifles.

The city centre was crowded with Yanks, wandering in pairs, in groups, congregating outside the most notorious pubs they had taken over from petty criminals, barrowboys and prostitutes. When Ernie and I ventured into town, we gawped at them admiringly as they shouted after giggling girls tripping down the street on their way to the Palais de Danse or the cinema, calling across the traffic to each other in Twentieth Century Fox drawls. Noisy, confident, swaggering in uniforms which could have been designed for a musical, they were more exotic than the Canadians, more foreign and mysterious. To Ernie and me they all looked like film stars, crooners or gangsters. My romantic image of them, nurtured by hours spent in the Forum, was probably shared by the girls who made a living on sewing machines or making cigarettes, girls from the depressing cobbled streets of the old suburbs. At first, the girls who had the nerve to go out with them were regarded as "common", for it was considered promiscuous by older women for a young girl to be seen with a Yank's arm around her waist, especially if he was black, although that was rare. I wondered what the Yanks thought of drab Nottingham, its miles of terraced houses and its rough pubs, as well as of the common accent of its citizens. I imagined that they must have found Nottingham a squalid place after Broadway, Fifth Avenue and Los Angeles. My optimism that these careless, sharply dressed and charismatic young men were about to drag us out of the torpor we had fallen into was derived from Mam's opinion of them. "They're leary sods," she said. "But they'll win the war for us."

Further evidence that the war was moving to a climax was provided by the roar of Lancaster bombers passing over Broxtowe on their journeys east. They were not in tight formation but massed, swarm-like, black against the late afternoon sky, thrilling us with their chorus of Merlin engines. I tried to count them as I walked home from school, but there were always too many of them and I lost count before they disappeared over the horizon. I never thought of the people who would die that night under their bombs. Germany was too remote, a name merely – the name of the enemy we had been taught to despise. There would be reports in the newspapers, and on the cinema newsreels, of raids on Essen, Dortmund and Frankfurt. But they, too, were just names. It was hard to imagine their citizens as individuals, and even harder to imagine them as people like us.

One afternoon the bombers flew over while we were still at our desks listening to Mr Garland, our geography teacher, droning from a text book while we fidgeted, waiting for the home-time bell. He stopped reading to listen, as we all did, as a kind of dumb homage when the familiar roar of engines approached. When the air was quiet again he said: "I am proud to be British today", and it seemed as noble a thing to say as Henry the Fifth's speech before Agincourt in the Laurence Olivier film we had been taken to see by the teachers, and which we half-understood as being somehow patriotic and defiant.

Such incidents were the prologue to the climactic invasion I had waited for with the same kind of stomach-fluttering anticipation that I felt before a fist fight. Still without a radio at home, I learned of the Normandy landings on D-Day from a classmate on my way to school. We argued in chirpy excitement about how long it would take us and the Yanks to reach Berlin. Now that the promised end was in sight we could talk of nothing but the war and the capture of Adolf Hitler and his gang of comic loons. We were too absorbed by the newspaper reports and the newsreels to anticipate what our lives might be like when there was no war. The revenge we dreamed of had arrived, and had to be savoured – every bloodstained moment of it.

But as we had slept that morning, the American paratroopers from the Wollaton Hall camp drifted down in darkness into the annihilation waiting for them as they fell upon a crack German infantry which Allied intelligence hadn't known about. Only 800 men returned to the camp at Wollaton out of a force of 2,000. Disasters, defeats like Dunkirk, the Blitz on London and Coventry, Cousin Tommy's desertion: they were hard to fit into my simple concept of war as an heroic activity, a conflict between the wholly good and the wholly evil. I thought that the Germans deserved what we were doing to their cities and to their army. But when I saw the Universal News shots of dead German soldiers looking like bundles of filthy rags as they lay beside their blazing lorries and tanks – saw their faces drained of life, I felt sorry for them, perhaps sensing for the first time what war *really* meant in terms of other people's suffering.

* * *

Before the invasion had begun, Mam had to placate Aunt Mabel again when she was dizzy with panic. Uncle Herbert was with the Allied force which landed on the lethal Anzio beachhead in Italy. The British army suffered heavy casualties under a devastating barrage of German artillery. My aunt daren't read the newspaper reports, and dreaded the sight of a telegraph boy cycling down the street in case he delivered a curt notification that her genial husband was dead, or missing. Uncle Herbert and his truck survived the ordeal unscathed, but when D-Day arrived, it was Mam's turn to be anxious. Dad was a member of a tank crew, now, and it was only a question of time before he became part of the invasion force in France. He told Mam that he didn't trust his driver whom, he felt, lacked skill. Dad had worked as a chauffeur before he became a bus-conductor, and was nervous if he wasn't at the controls. "Some of 'em drive like madheads," he complained when he came home on leave. His scepticism was finally justified when he was crewman to a learner who lost control of the tank while they were on an exercise. The panic-stricken learner tried to jump out of the tank as it rolled over on a bank, and was crushed to death. True to his nature, Dad obeyed the instructions to stay inside the tank in such a situation. It saved his life, although the violent motions threw him around helplessly, fracturing his skull. There was little detail in the diplomatic letter Mam received from his C.O. Dad's injuries were serious, but he would recover. He had been unconscious for 36 hours, but had now come round. Bombardier Buttress was a good soldier, one valued by his officers. Mam was welcome to visit him in hospital, and could stay as long as she liked – the army would arrange accommodation.

Aunt Mabel came to the rescue: she lent Mam a suitcase and a decent navy-blue costume. Then she moved in to look after Brenda, Peter and me while Mam was away. I remember feeling relief that Dad would now miss the rest of the war as a front-line soldier. Those blast-torn, dehumanized figures lying in stiff postures of death that denied all human dignity, and which I saw for a brief moment on the screen of the Forum, would not include Dad. He would be spared that humiliation, and I no longer imagined his glum face among the faces of dead soldiers on grainy newsreel film.

Chapter 19

Soldier's Return

After he was discharged from the army on medical grounds, Dad said nothing about his experience as a soldier, or about his brush with death. In keeping with his secretive nature, he revealed little of his past to anyone. As far as he was concerned his accident was history, now. All I knew of his life was what I observed myself, or what I overheard when Mam talked about him. But even she didn't know what kind of boy he had been, or what memories of youth stayed with him. If he had once been ambitious he never spoke about it, nor did he give the slightest indication that any part of his life had a particular significance. Whatever he might have had in the way of dreams and expectations was locked away, or perhaps forgotten. It was as if he was reluctant to give any more of himself than he had to as a father and a husband. He was like a miser, his past a personal possession he secreted behind long, mournful periods of silence. He tried to be a father, and he was probably faithful as a husband, but that was as much as he was prepared to give of himself. He could never be a friend to me, or much of a companion to Mam because that would be giving too much of himself, and he didn't know how.

I picked up random details of his childhood from Grandma Buttress. The most surprising was the picture she drew of him as a boy sitting on a wall on Hollis Street practising a harmonica she had bought him. What was less surprising was that he always told passers-by to "clear off!" if they stopped to listen to him. She related how her quiet, well-behaved home-loving boy had made Charlie Chaplin his hero. He began to copy Chaplin's comic walk, and this worried her because it was anything but comic when he was out shopping with her. He was a solitary boy who never ventured far from the house, one who was afraid of his father, and worshipped his mother. Throughout his life he was committed to that mother-love, his weekly visits to her meaning more to him, I am sure, than his wife, children, work and duty. His grief when she died in her eighties was profound. It was the only time I saw him cry, and he was sixty years old then. Dad rarely spoke of his own father except to complain about the old man's disparaging remarks about soldiers of Dad's generation compared to the army of the Great War. Yet when Grandad was made helpless by a severe stroke, and lay motionless in a bed brought down into the parlour, the dutiful, cowed son shaved the old man then sat by him, speaking rarely, but with a gentleness that perplexed me. The son in him was a revelation. He displayed a depth of feeling I had never witnessed in him before – so brusque, even harsh, was his attitude towards me most of the time.

Mam went to collect him when he was discharged from the military hospital. A doctor informed her that Dad's nerves would probably be affected by the trauma of the accident. His behaviour might be unpredictable, his moods depressive. When Mam told me what the doctor had said my heart sank, as hers must have done. How much more depressively moody could he be? Our family life revolved around his moods *before* he was called up for service in the army. They determined the atmosphere in the house, the tone of our conversations, even our very actions. When he was in bed we tip-toed about the house in case we woke him into a bad mood; when he came home from the pub or work we read his face anxiously. The look in his eyes, the set of his mouth told us all that we needed to know about how to conduct ourselves: was it safe to laugh or even talk? Or was it best to observe a diplomatic silence?

Both Mam and I expected the worst, but we underestimated his innate powers of survival. He pushed the accident, the death of his mate, and even his short service in the army to the back of his mind, where so much of his past lay. He got on with his tight-lipped life, commenting only on the skinflint pension the government awarded him for his injury. The only evidence of the trauma was that he was even more silent than usual in the weeks following his return. He eased himself back into our lives with the quiet deliberation of a man intent on achieving anonymity. He brushed aside inquiries about his health from neighbours, sisters and Radfords with an edgy politeness. Mam kept her distance with painstaking reserve – quite an achievement for her. When she spoke to him her guarded tone conveyed her wariness of his state of mind. So tentative and unnatural was the atmosphere in the house that I was relieved, almost happy, when Dad lost his temper with me for the first time since his return home. Here, at last, was the man we recognized as Dad. We now knew when it was diplomatic to speak, and when it was best to keep quiet.

I must have grown wild and undisciplined while he was away in spite of Mam's punishing slaps, cuffs, rollickings and explosive temper. I no longer took much notice of her chastisement. Her responses to my misdemeanours, real or imagined, were too familiar. They were also transitory. Ten minutes after a slap on the head and being called "a leary sod", because I had answered back cheekily, she would send me down to the shops for five Woodbine, or to Brady and Barber with a bet on the horses with the promise of a treat to the Forum if her nags came up. A row with Mam was democratic, egalitarian. I was allowed my say, too, if I was prepared to take the risk of it ending with a slap. When I judged that her temper was approaching boiling point, I would make a dash for the door, and a hurried exit into the back garden. If I was too slow to escape, I had to take the hard slap, usually at the back of the head, a signal that democracy was ended for the day, the argument over. But her slaps didn't really hurt any longer, and her swearing was only effective if it was emphasized by her throwing one of my library books, or a small ornament at me.

Dad would have regarded any attempt to argue with him as anarchy, a defiance of authority he would not allow. His notion of a father-son relationship was founded upon his own submissive one with Grandad Buttress. I never argued with Dad because I was too scared of him. He rarely slapped me; a cold, disheartening, ego-diminishing look from him was enough to wither me into submission. When he did raise his voice to me the underlying message was short, clear, and immutable: "I will tell you to do something. You will do it. I am your father". And I obeyed. Nearly always.

156

He set about the task of trying to repair the damage my freedom from his influence had wrought on my character. He began with my appearance, an immediate source of irritation. I was generally scruffy, even before I went out to meet Ernie and Mo. When I came home after roving through woods and fields with them, I would be dirty and torn, too. "Look at the state of you!" he always raged. "You're like a big, soft kid. God knows how you get into that mess. Get washed and up to kip!" Other flaws in my character were picked out and punished in the same way. "It's time you did a bit more in the house. And you can start getting to bed earlier. It's time you could mend your own shoes. I could do it when I was your age!" He was an expert cobbler and skilfully repaired all the family's shoes, having been taught such old-fashioned self-sufficiency by Grandad Buttress. "It's time you had more sense," he would rightly complain after I had ruined his handiwork by playing football until the uppers of my shoes split.

It was always time to have more sense: always time to be more serious, responsible, dutiful. But, approaching thirteen years of age, I had a hazy, self-protective notion that time was on my side before I became as cowed as he was before his own father. With luck, I thought, and a bit of cheek, I'll never become like Dad, although I had no idea who I wanted to be like. I was beginning to realize that the distance between us might be due to the fact that I was as much a Radford as I was a Buttress. Perhaps he feared that I might grow up as uncouth as Tommy, and that was what made him snap and snarl at me.

The rows between Mam and Dad didn't begin again until he had been home for several months. The peace was broken when Dad felt strong enough to start work. He turned down the offer of his old job on the corporation buses and went to work at a small engineering factory where Mam also had a job. His disregard for Mam's financial problems surfaced again when he brought his first pay packet home. When he was a bus conductor, she had always known what he earned because the wage was advertized in the vacancies column of the *Evening Post*. But now, even though they worked together in the same factory, his wage became the best-kept secret of the war. No amount of probing, cajoling or head-on demanding by Mam would get him to reveal how much spending money he stuffed into his pocket on a Friday night. The old resentments were reignited, and the shouting began. Her constant complaints about the struggle to manage on her housekeeping allowance led to fierce, contemptuous battles of their stubborn wills when he took his generous share of his wages down to the pubs on Hyson Green, his old haunts, to play dominoes and cards.

Later, he went to work at the Raleigh Cycle factory where the work was numbingly repetitive. The operators functioned as part of the machine, and physical endurance was the main requirement from them. They were numbers on a clocking-in card, automatons serving the endless chain which carried thousands of cycle parts from one part of the plant to another. Pubs were an anaesthetic, the relief towards which Dad and his mates plodded through the long, wearisome tunnel of the working week. He wasn't a big drinker: I never saw him drunk, and he never allowed his self-protective guard to fall. Nor did he become maudlin enough to display the temporary bonhomie which would earn me a reckless shilling from Uncle George, Cousin Tommy or Uncle Herbert when they had had a good night on Shipstone's mild beer. The only indication Dad gave of having been to the pub was to bring home a keen appetite for his dinner after a Sunday lunch-time session, and a "kip" in bed before the evening session began.

Mam sometimes accompanied him on Saturday nights, a row beginning before they even set off because she knew by the downcast look on his face that he was reluctant to take her. Dad had been nurtured on Grandad's ethic that life was largely a burden, one to be suffered as a father and a husband. A man was to work for and support a family. But he was to be allowed his privacy, that was his right because he was a man. What went off inside the family was his business. The family might be a woman's favourite topic of conversation, but for men of Dad's generation, social life was more satisfying, especially when it was within the circle of other men. Later, I discovered that he was only at ease with a pub-bar crowd around a table where the dominoes rattled and the cards were dealt in a tense game of brag or pontoon. There was no pressure in that smoky, beer-fumed, club-like atmosphere, no wives or kids or bosses clamouring for your time, your energy or your life. When Mam insisted that he take her with him on the week's big night out, Dad was miserable because she was the ball and chain he was trying to slip free of.

Anxious about her debts, fuming at Dad's contempt of her inability to manage her money, Mam watched through a cold silence as he examined his clean, white collar then dressed in his neat, meticulous fashion before strolling off to catch a bus to the pub. If he went out of the house alone, Mam would shout after him: "I hope you fall under a bus!", and Brenda and I would know that we were in for a stormy Saturday night when he got back from the pub.

The worst rows were always after a Saturday night session, especially if Dad had left Mam at home to fume at his selfishness. I lay in bed in the darkness, my hands over my ears as the raging voices rose from the living-room. Sometimes there was shuffling as though they were fighting, a chair knocked over, a pot smashing, Mam crying. Then I would go to the head of the stairs and shout down to them to stop, over and over, until Dad would come into the hall, yelling at Mam to "shut your rattle!" before he shouted up to me to get back to bed. I would do as he said, but lay there with tears burning on my face because of what they were doing to themselves, to Brenda and to me.

* * *

I followed Mam and Dad's private war as I cringed under my bedclothes vainly trying to shut it out. The public war I studied in comparative tranquillity from the newspapers. Its battles were reassuringly distant and impersonal, and could be shut out at any time. The accounts of death and destruction on the mainland of Europe were only slightly more real than the war films I enjoyed at the Forum. An air-raid on Broxtowe was highly unlikely now that Hitler was on the brink of defeat, even though the newspapers told of a new terror that he was inflicting on London – the V1 "Doodlebugs" and the V2 rockets. London was a long way off, we thought, and the war hardly touched us now that Dad was home. The ridiculous appellation "Doodlebug" itself reduced the awful reality of the weapon for my Withern Road pals and me. How could you be scared of a pilotless plane called a "Doodlebug"? It sounded like something out of the pages of the *Dandy*.

The reality was made manifest, though, when a bus-load of evacuees fleeing from the last-ditch bombardment of London was driven into Broxtowe. Dusk was beginning to encroach on our play, and some of the younger kids had already wandered home, when a single-decker bus pulled up by the green on Withern Road. Ernie, Mo and I abandoned our game and raced across the green to see what had brought this unusual visitation, for no bus had ever been seen on the road before. Other kids joined us, until there were about a dozen of us crowding around the bus, peering in at the windows. It was half-full of women and children, most of them standing in the aisle peering back at us with tired, frightened faces. A grey haired, well dressed man carrying a megaphone stepped down from the platform of the bus. He was followed by two women who wore armbands indicating that they were members of the W.V.S. They hurried off to the nearest houses to knock on front doors.

"What's up, mate?" Ernie asked.

"We're looking for people to take in these ladies and their children for the night. They've been travelling all day. Can your parents take anybody?"

The appeal was to all of us, but only Ernie responded by shooting home across the green. The rest of us stared through the bus windows at the anxious faces staring back bleakly, perhaps resentful of our curiosity. Women came out of the houses following the W.V.S. workers. The man with the megaphone wrote their names and addresses onto a clipboard. The mothers and children struggled out of the bus with bags and bulging suitcases to follow the women to their houses. Ernie ran back to report that there was no room in his house, a fact which had been obvious to the rest of the gang.

Eventually, only one family was left on the bus: a plain-looking woman in a shabby coat that was so loose on her it looked as if it had been given to her by somebody two sizes bigger. Two toddlers clung to the coat, and she had a baby in her arms which was fast asleep. The man began to walk down the middle of the road, the bus crawling after him. We trotted on the pavement, keeping up with the bus to stare through the dirty windows at the woman, this weary looking visitor from the real war.

160

"We have one more family!" the man shouted through the megaphone. "One more family ... Can somebody take one more family?" He looked exhausted.

There was no offer of a haven for the night for the woman. The hospitality on Withern Road had been fully exploited. The man waited for the bus to catch up with him, then he hopped onto the platform. It was almost dark as the bus picked up speed and we had to run fast along the pavement to keep up. The woman with the children appeared to be crying, one of the W.V.S. women comforting her with an arm around her shoulder. The bus pulled away, and we stopped running, watching it in silence as it turned a corner. No-one spoke as we walked back to the green, all of us, perhaps, shamed by our intrusive stares at the woman with nowhere to sleep.

Hurrying home on my own, I wondered if the man with the megaphone had found someone charitable enough to welcome the woman and her children. I realized that I knew so little about the reality of the war. Broxtowe was so secure, so far away from where the real suffering was taking place. The war had ceased to be exciting. Now it was just a sad, grinding drawn-out drama that played on and on even when everybody was sick of it. Home isn't much, I thought, but it's there, and we're safe. I didn't even mind too much when Dad snapped at me for being late.

Chapter 20

My German

Ernie cast his maggot onto the black, oil-filmed surface of Wollaton canal and watched it slowly sink with a flick of his home-made bamboo fishing rod. Behind us the headstock of Wollaton pit was an intricate silhouette against the pearly light, the angles of the ramshackle buildings huddled close to it softened by the hazy sun. Earlier in the century, coal from the pit was transported on the canal, now both were obsolete. That Spring of 1945 was to be the last that Ernie and I would spent together as close friends, though neither of us suspected it, then. On our way to the canal we had scrumped a few apples wasting on the old trees of Moor Farm, left-overs from the previous Autumn. They would help to quell our hunger pangs, for we intended to stay out until tea-time. The half-rotten fruit lay on a patch of spring grass poking through the cinder towpath. Ernie hardly ever caught a fish here, but that didn't matter. Fishing was an excuse to laze away an afternoon. The fishing rod could be left to look after itself while we did a spot of bird-nesting or Ernie went for a swim. He was at the end of his schooldays. Soon he would start work at Babbington pit which lay a downhill mile from Broxtowe. If his childhood was over, officially, Ernie welcomed it. He looked forward to becoming a miner, a man, and that would take place as an instant transformation the second he donned a miner's helmet. He had even started to practise chewing tobacco, although it made him retch. He had expected it to taste like liquorice.

I slipped my hand into the water, feeling the slime on the stone supporting the lock gate. The canal was a good place for tadpoles and frogs, but it was too early for them yet. They thrived here because the

162

water was tepidly warm. Somewhere higher up, water from the old pit was pumped into the canal, and that made it a favourite place for swimming. All the lads from the estate called this stretch of the canal the "hotties". No decent sized fish could survive here because of the pollution from the pit, and Ernie knew it.

Beyond the fields stretching toward the outskirts of Nottingham lay the ornamental pinnacles of Wollaton Hall. The Yanks had gone. Now the site was enclosed by high barbed-wire fencing behind which stood the long wooden huts housing German prisoners of war. All around lay the flat fields of Wollaton and Bilborough, their days as farmland drawing to a close after a thousand years. The post-war years would see their acres packed with council houses until the ancient villages were completely surrounded by them, the woods bulldozed and the hawthorn hedges burned. That morning, though, the blackbirds still sang in the old fox covets and the shoots of nettles and wild blackberry showed by the side of the towpath. By the time all this new growth had died back under the frosts of Winter I, too, would be at work. The event seemed a long way off and didn't disturb me yet. It lay beyond the Summer, my final term at school, and probably the end of the war.

I lay on my elbow and bit through a wormy apple, enjoying the first warmth of the year. Ernie's float shivered slightly on the surface of an oil rainbow patch in the middle of the canal. The quivering would be caused by minnows, so Ernie ignored it. He took out his old lozenge tin and rolled himself a cigarette in a Rizla paper with tobacco saved from his old nub ends, supplemented by those he had collected from the gutters on our way here. When he became a man the first thing he planned to do was to march into Purdy's the newsagent and demand ten Woodbine.

"Let's try somewhere else," I suggested. I was bored. I didn't have the patience required for fishing. I always resisted Ernie's suggestion that I make a rod for myself. Watching an idle float for hours on end was not my idea of fun. "We could walk to Martin's pond," I nagged.

Ernie drew on his ragged cigarette. "Nah. There's pike in this spot. They like the warm water." He knew as well as I did that a pike in the dirty old canal would probably be there to commit suicide. He knew, also, that the only life supported by the canal was tadpoles, insects, snails and stinking green slime. The biggest thing Ernie ever hauled out of Wollaton canal was a bike frame. I didn't challenge his fanciful theory about pike because I had just noticed a canvas-topped army truck parked by the side of the building close to the headstock of the pit. I was glad of the distraction and rolled onto my stomach to gaze at it. I wondered what an army truck was doing in the pit yard when half-a-dozen German prisoners of war in grey uniforms emerged from a ramshackle cabin armed with sweeping brushes and shovels. They began to sweep the yard, making little piles of dust and small coal which they shovelled up to toss onto a waste heap. They were supervised by a skinny, thin-faced British corporal with a swagger stick jammed under his armpit as though he was a general on inspection.

"Hey, look – Germans" I informed Ernie.

He rolled over onto his stomach to watch. "Yeah, them's the bastards," he said, pulling on the wet stub of his disintegrating cigarette. "Them's Jerries alright. The only good Jerry is a dead'un," he said, echoing an observation I had heard his dad make many times. "Heil Hitler!" Ernie shouted at the figures labouring in the yard, placing a finger under his nose to simulate Hitler's comic moustache, and lifting his arm in a Nazi salute.

"Shurrup!" I poked him with my elbow. "They'll hear you!"

"I'm not frightened of 'em." Ernie said. "Hey up kraut – how big's your sausage?" he yelled.

One of the Germans, a young man, looked up, a puzzled expression on his face as though he was wondering where the shout came from. He spotted us, then lifted his hand in greeting.

"He's heard you," I said, a bit worried.

"So what? He's only a Jerry," Ernie said, although he sounded less confident now. "D'you reckon they're Nazis?"

"I thought they were all Nazis." As far as I was concerned the words "German" and "Nazi" were synonymous. I put it down to Ernie's lack of education that he thought a German might not be a Nazi.

"They don't look up to much," Ernie scoffed. "No wonder they lost the war."

"It's not over yet," I reminded him.

164

"Where's the soldier's rifle?" He nodded towards the British corporal who was leaning on the tailboard of the truck as he watched the lethargic prisoners at their work. Judging by their slow movement it was easy to see that they were bored by the task.

"One of our soldiers to look after all them," Ernie commented as though it proved the superiority of the British army. "And he's only got a bleeding stick."

The young German took out a pack of cigarettes then strolled over to the corporal, offered him one, and they both lit up. The guard nodded as though the German had asked him a question. They both looked in our direction, then the prisoner slowly walked towards us.

"Bogger me – he's coming over here!" Ernie said.

As he got close I was surprised at how youthful he looked. He smiled uncertainly as he eased himself down beside us, sitting cross-legged on the narrow strip of grass bordering the canal. My first German! He looked nothing like the bullet-headed apes in all those war films I had watched at the Forum. He was slim, fair haired with eyes of an intense blue. When he spoke, however, I was gratified that Hollywood had got the German accent right at least.

"Not good river," he ventured, tossing a pebble into the water. "Not good for fishing."

"Don't throw things in the water," Ernie said tetchily. "I'm after a pike."

I glanced at the tiny ripples his pebble had made. "It's not a river. It's a canal," I explained, not wanting him to think all English rivers were black, stagnant and rainbow filmed with oil.

"A canal?" The German looked bemused.

"No flow ... Water stand still. No flow like river!" I raised my voice as I thought necessary with a foreigner, then I weaved my hand through the air to demonstrate the liquidity of running water. I decided that he would understand better if I assumed the accent of a Hollywood German. "We have good river. Many fish. River Trent is our river." I pointed in the general direction of Wollaton Hall. "Over there. About three mile."

"I know River Trent," he said, smiling, perhaps amused because I was shouting.

"Where're you from?" I inquired. I knew the names of all the towns in the Ruhr valley with the R.A.F. had bombed.

"I live in Koln – you say Cologne. Koln is very nice place. My river there is very clean. I fish many time. Better than this." He tossed another pebble into the canal then drew on his cigarette before tossing it away. Ernie gave him a dirty look, although I wasn't sure whether it was for frightening his imaginary pike, or for wasting half a cigarette. I, also, was a bit piqued by his criticism of our neglected "cut".

"What you do in pit?" Ernie demanded, having learned the accent from seeing the same war films as me. "I work in pit soon."

"We do many job, but very dirty. Gardening is best job. Pit work is too rough."

Ernie sulked at this disparaging reference to his future, sitting up to pull his maggot out of the water for inspection.

"You catch fish?" the German asked.

"Not yet. Catch big pike soon," Ernie fibbed. He glared at the maggot as though its idleness was unpatriotic before tossing it back into the water.

"Where you learn English?" I asked.

"In school. Not good in English."

"You speak it well," I flattered.

"Not good," he insisted, smiling again.

"What's it like being a Nazi?" Ernie suddenly demanded, probably out of spite.

A frown crossed the German's face, a pained look which made him appear angry. "I am not Nazi. Many people in Koln not Nazi. My family hate Hitler. We want war to end. Nazis are bad people."

He brooded for a minute, his eyes focused on Ernie's float, his mind obviously somewhere else. It had never occurred to me that a German could be capable of hating Hitler, and of hating the war. I believed him instantly because he looked so miserable.

"What is your name?" he asked of Ernie as though he was trying to erase the thought that had silenced him.

Ernie told him, the German repeating it accurately, then he glanced at me. "My name's Derrick," I said, and he repeated that perfectly too.

166

"My name is Karl," he said.

"Do you want some apples? We've got plenty. They're a bit scabby, though."

"Scabby? What is 'scabby'?"

"Old. Last year's. A bit bad." I picked out the least weather and grub damaged specimens. He smiled when I handed them to him, perhaps understanding why they were offered. "Thank you," he said. "Apples are good."

The clang of shovels being tossed into the back of the army truck jolted our attention towards the pit yard. One of the Germans was staring at us from the edge of the newly swept area. He was thick-set, much older than Karl, and wore glasses which looked metal-rimmed, or were frameless. He lit the stub of a cigar, never taking his eyes off us. How could he be allowed the luxury of a cigar? I had never seen any of the men in our family smoke a cigar. He could have stepped down from the screen of the Forum as my archetypal Hollywood German, the thick-necked Hun of "B" films. If I hadn't been so nervous under his stare I would have laughed at this parody casually smoking his cigar as though he owned the place. Karl saw him and lowered his eyes, brushing cinder dust from his grey trousers. "Don't look," he said in a quiet voice. "He makes trouble. I should not talk to you. I go now."

"Is he a Nazi?" Ernie asked, shielding his eyes to get a better look.

"Yes. He is Nazi," Karl said. He got to his feet, cradling the apples in the crook of his arm. "I go back to camp now. Thank you for apples. Have good fishing." He nodded, then strode off towards the pit yard.

The corporal hit the tailboard of the truck with his swagger stick, impatient to get his prisoners loaded. The cigar-smoking German muttered something to Karl as he passed him, but the young man ignored him and made straight for the truck, climbing in awkwardly still clutching the apples. The older German tossed his cigar butt into nettles at the edge of the yard then followed the rest of the prisoners, climbing into the back of the truck. The corporal fastened two chains on the tailboard before walking round to the cab, rapping his stick on the side to indicate to the driver that their prisoners were secure. He climbed into the cab, the engine coughed into life and the truck moved forward.

As it negotiated the tight passage between the dilapidated buildings Ernie and I watched in silence. I would never see him again, and I wanted to know why he wasn't a Nazi if he was a German. He was nothing like my uncles and cousins. Somehow he seemed more refined: if he had been English he would have been "posh", but he was friendly all the same. I would like to have known him better, but I never would now. Before the truck disappeared beyond the buildings we saw the apples fly out of the back to bounce on the cinder roadway.

"That'll be the Nazi," Ernie said, perhaps relieved that his patriotic assumptions about the degeneracy of the German nation were confirmed by the rejection of the innocent apples. "All Nazis are rotten."

"Karl was alright," I said.

Ernie shrugged. "He wasn't bad for a Jerry." He turned back to the canal to watch his float twitching under a new attack by the minnows.

I walked into a scalding attack from Mam when I wandered into the house after our fishless expedition. Ernie had finally become so irate by the tantalizing quiver of his float as the minnows lunched on his maggot that he decided to go for a swim instead. The towpath was too public for naked swimming, so he dived into the canal wearing his underpants. He had to dry off naturally as he had no towel. Of course, his underpants wouldn't dry on him, so he took them off when there was no-one in sight, carrying them home hanging from the end of his fishing road.

I was famished when I got to Broxtowe, having given the larger part of our makeshift dinner to the German. I had expected my tea to be laid out on the table when I stepped into the kitchen, but was met by an angry fusilade from Mam.

"Where the bleddy hell have you been all this time?" she shouted.

"Out," I answered brazenly, foolishly ignoring the angry scowl on her face.

"I'll bleddy 'out' you, you cheeky sod!" She took a swipe at me, but I was adept at swaying from her clumsy assaults.

"What've I done?" I complained, defensive now. "I've only been down the canal."

"I'll bleddy canal you!" she threatened.

Sometimes Mam's oaths and threats were so illogical that I found it hard to suppress a laugh, which would only get me into more trouble. If she hadn't been so mad I might have summoned up the nerve to ask what being "canalled" meant, but realized that such leary nit-picking would only drive her into a more dangerous anger.

"What've I done? I haven't done anything!" It was time to play the innocent, an appropriate tone of hurt in my voice.

"It's what you haven't done ... I've been waiting for you to go to the shops for his tea. He'll be here in half an hour." "He" was Dad.

"Why can't Brenda go? It's always me that has to go."

"Brenda does enough, that's why. And have less of your lip!"

The errand lay between me and my tea, so off I flew to the Co-op. When I got back, quickly, for I ran all the way, she was mollified, her volcano merely smouldering, and by setting the table without being asked I crawled back into favour. We were enjoying a period of peace in the house. Mam was well into another pregnancy, a condition which guaranteed a temporary lull in the warfare between my parents. The occasional row flared, but never amounted to much. Dad suppressed his worse rages out of deference to Mam's handicap in what was, normally, an equal battle.

"You'd better get yourself washed before he sees you in that state," she warned as I set out knives and forks with grime encrusted hands. "And get your shoes cleaned as well."

"I talked to a Jerry today," I informed her as I swilled under the kitchen tap. "His name was Karl."

"You stand need to talk to Jerries," she responded enigmatically.

"He was alright, though. He wasn't a Nazi."

"How do you know? He wouldn't tell you if he was."

"He said he wasn't. He didn't look like one. Not like them you see in films."

I didn't tell her about the other German. I didn't know how to describe him without making him seen ridiculously melodramatic, an imaginary baddie from an R.K.O. movie. "This German was alright.

He lives in Cologne, only he called it something else. His family don't like Hitler."

Mam had gone quiet. She turned a chop over in the frying pan. I thought she was tired of my prattle, or preoccupied with timing Dad's tea so that it would be ready for the table the moment he stepped through the door. "He'll be some mother's son," she said at last, and that was what she always said of young men who were dead, injured or in trouble, perhaps signifying her empathy with those whom life chose as its victims.

* * *

I thought about Karl for weeks afterwards – even worried about him, wondering if the German with the cigar had made trouble for him because he spoke to us. The war had gradually become defined in my mind as a group of unconnected individuals, linked only by what the war had done to them: the sobbing woman on the evacuee bus; the husband of Aunt Mabel's friend, a slow talking, rather gormless soldier who had been burned to death tending the smoke-screen oil drums in Radford; the Yank Tommy knocked out in the pub on Hyson Green when he was in a black mood; a Canadian soldier I saw carried, bleeding and semi-conscious, into the rent office after he came off his dispatch-rider motorbike; the death of Joe Peach. I wanted the war to end because it perpetuated such small tragedies, so small most of them didn't even get a mention in the *Evening Post*, but which were the biggest tragedies of all to me because they were part of my life, now, were established in my memory. Now I wanted Karl to see his family again in that place with the funny name, which we called Cologne, and to which the Lancaster bombers roared in the late afternoon.

Newsreels were two dimensional, second-hand and transitory. The black and white images on the screen of the Forum aroused a few seconds of regret and compassion in spite of the strident commentary that accompanied them. But the newsreel was followed by a Hollywood fantasy in which even violent death was presented as an entertainment, a storybook triumph of good over evil. The hero in a western would kill half a dozen men in a shoot-out, and the bodies

170

would just lie there with nobody taking any notice of them. It always struck me as deeply immoral that characters could stand about talking, unconcerned, smiling, while dead men littered the floor. Mam's saying always came into my mind: "They'll be some mothers' sons," and that always made me feel uneasy. The suffering shown by the newsreels became just another story, one set in a distant place, its inhabitants no more than extras, as unreal as those in most movies. But Karl had come within touching distance. I had heard him laugh, no matter how briefly. Now I knew what lay behind those empty masks of death worn by German soldiers in the newsreels. And like Aunt Mabel, I had come to hate the war.

Chapter 21

This England

Arthur Smith, our mercurial English teacher, bald, dandyish and with the ascetic face of a ham actor, led his flock of choral verse performers up the steps of the grandiose Council House. We would have followed him anywhere, such was his charisma. The building dominated the Nottingham skyline. Built in 1928 to a pseudo classical design in white Portland stone, it looked like a huge iced cake topped by a weather-stained dome as if somebody had put a lid on it to protect the confectionary from the rain, and from diarrhoeic pigeons. Most people in Nottingham loved it, as I did, as a building which gave an illusion of grandeur, rising high above the more homely Edwardian buildings which surrounded it. It also gave the tired city a focus, something to look up to even though it might be merely to check the time by its enormous clock whose deep-toned bell, called Little John, we could hear striking as far away as Broxtowe.

Smith hushed our excited chatter as he led us into the foyer from which rose a wide sweep of stairs through white marble banisters. As we stood gawping at its richness, a uniformed usher with a glinting display of Great War medals on his chest approached us. "The Player School choral verse group," Smith announced theatrically. The usher grinned, perhaps because we didn't look very poetical, then nodded towards the Busby Berkeley staircase. We spoke in whispers as we ascended, one or two of us giggling with stage fright. An official met us at the top of the stairs, smiled pleasantly in greeting before leading us into a large reception room. Doric columns supported a high ceiling from which hung chandeliers that might have graced a Hollywood film set. At one end of the room there was a row of French-windows, and beyond them a long, balustraded balcony which extended along the front of the building. Below lay the wide expanse of the Market Square, an arrangement of steps between walled flower beds which had been excavated to build reservoirs for use in an emergency by the fire brigade.

"Have some refreshment," the official said. "You have about ten minutes. We'll wait until Little John's struck so that it doesn't interrupt your performance."

We crowded around a table big enough to hold a banquet. It was covered by a dazzling white cloth on which was laid large jugs of lemonade and plates piled high with fancy biscuits. We helped ourselves with as much restraint as we thought proper for the occasion, but in five minutes we had cleared the table of its unexpected feast. "You haven't left much for the Lord Mayor," the official said, mock serious, then he and Smith laughed at our guilty faces.

We had rehearsed John of Gaunt's speech from Shakespeare's *Richard the Second* especially for the celebrations of Victory in Europe Day because it propagated the idea that England was some sort of paradise, and worth fighting for. Arthur Smith was a missionary of choral verse speaking, preaching the message wherever he could that even the roughest of boys would respond to poetry if it was played as a team game. We enjoyed doing it because it got us out of lessons. We even went on a trip by train to Leicester to demonstrate our skill to an audience of bored-looking teachers. With his usual zeal, Smith had approached the Education Department and won us the gig at the Council House as part of the city's celebrations. We were fitted in at the dog-end of the week's programme of events, but our spot was too early in the morning to attract much attention from the few people who crossed the Market Square.

On V.E. Day itself I had been down in the Square with Billy, a pal from school. He was as interested in girls as I was. We jumped off the bus from Broxtowe and threw ourselves into the melee of revellers jammed into the Square. Dance music blared from the balcony of the Council House. Most of the celebrating servicemen were dancing, some even embraced two girls at a time and grinned at their mates.

When Billy and I saw a couple of unattached girls elbowing their way through a fox-trot in front of the Council House steps we would push through the crowd to reach them, follow them around like a couple of love-hungry dopes in the hope of discovering what it would be like to hold hands with a girl we didn't know, or even kiss one. The trouble was, neither Billy nor I had the faintest idea about how to dance. "Clear off!" one of the prettier girls shouted as we trailed them from one end of the Square to the other. "We don't go out with idiots!" Billy and I realised, then, that wrestling with each other to demonstrate our toughness was not the way to impress sophisticated girls like these.

We couldn't drag ourselves away to go home for tea, or supper, because the music was endless, like the dancing, the casual kissing and the smooching between the lucky servicemen and the excited girls. Billy and I watched and wondered at the joy of being a uniformed twenty-year old instead of an unregarded schoolboy. But how could we leave in the middle of our first party, one to which the whole city had invited itself? The music was endless. The girls laughed just because they were there, caught up in the wonder of it all. One or two of them laughed at us in a way that we mistook for an invitation, so we fought our way through the crowd to keep them in sight without being able to pluck up the courage to speak to them. We had never enjoyed ourselves so much. "I've never seen so many birds!" Billy shouted. "There's millions of them! We're bound to get off with a couple soon!" And he tagged on to the end of the screaming conga snake of dancers hopping and kicking through the crowds jamming the pavements, the roads and the Square before returning, breathless, to the dance area in front of the Council House steps.

The day was hectic enough, but when the servicemen and their girls spilled out of the pubs around the Square in the evening the laughter grew louder, the kissing more passionate and the dancing more intimate as the crowds pushed the couples together. It seemed as if the revelry would go on for ever. Billy and I were held there, transfixed by such huge happiness in the middle of our work-a-day city. How could we leave such excitement, so many girls, and the disturbing possibility of winning a kiss or two? Finally, we missed the last bus home and had to walk the four miles back to Broxtowe, dizzy with the echoing music still in our ears.

Billy and I returned to the Square the next day, but the excitement had gone – swept up with the night's litter. We kept going back, joining those like ourselves who regretted the end of the party, a small crowd of youths and girls wandering among the pigeons as though we were searching for a lost joy. Bored, we sat on the steps of the Council House to watch those with a purpose hurrying by – the shoppers and the office girls, the errand boys and the shift workers crossing the Square, preoccupied with the depressing normality of it all, and ignoring the dance music still scratching away on the balcony. We were the disappointed witnesses to the demise of an excitement which had flared joyfully for a day and a night, then had expired in the sullen resumption of ordinary life. Finally, we left the Square to the old, the unemployed and the tramps lounging on the seats and gazing mournfully at everything and nothing, just as they had always done.

Now we were at the end of the week's celebrations organized by the City Council. At ten o'clock in the morning the Square looked depressingly indifferent. People with places to go and duties to perform crossed the forecourt in front of the Council House or hurried down the steps into the Square, passing those who had paused only to feed the flocks of smoky-feathered pigeons with crusts before moving on. After Little John had struck his hour, and the reverberations died away in the reception room, our choral verse group stepped out onto the balcony. The official spoke into a microphone, his voice echoing emptily from the buildings enclosing the Square. "Ladies and gentlemen, a group of lads from the Player School are going to entertain us with a bit of patriotic poetry. They'll remind us all just what it is we've been fighting for! Ladies and gentlemen, the John Player School choral verse group!"

There was no response from below. A hurrying figure might have glanced up to see where the noise was coming from, but no-one stopped, no-one welcomed us with the applause we had imagined would greet us. "It's great poetry, boys," Smith had told us in school. "It's music, so feel it! Don't see-saw – you aren't on a roundabout!" Actually, most of us thought it was corny, a bit embarrassing, like a

175

speech from some posh officer in a British war film such as *In Which We Serve*. I wondered where this England was that it spoke of, because I knew that it wasn't in Broxtowe, and all the men I knew, like Dad, weren't a very happy breed. In fact, they were downright bloody miserable. Smith liked the speech, though, and that made us determined to do our best for him. We began on his whispered cue: "one, two, three," in unison, attacking our consonants and fattening our skinny Nottingham vowels just as he had taught us.

> *This royal throne of Kings, this sceptred isle,*
> *This earth of majesty, this seat of Mars,*
> *This other Eden, demi-paradise,*
> *This fortress built by Nature for herself*
> *Against the infection and the hand of war,*
> *This happy breed of men, this little world,*
> *This precious stone set in the silver sea,*
> *Which serves in the office of a wall,*
> *Or as a moat defensive to a house,*
> *Against the envy of less happier lands;*
> *This blessed plot, this earth, this realm,*
>   *this England ...*

When we finished, the only sound we heard as the echo of our voices died away was the low whine of a trolley bus pulling away from its stop at the other end of the Square. I could see two women, who had met on the forecourt as we chanted our piece, deeply engrossed in the conversation they had begun. Pigeons scrabbled among the morning's crusts and crumbs throughout our painstaking performance. As we rode back to school on the bus we were subdued, disappointed, somehow feeling cheated. Nothing was how you imagined it would be. No matter what you dreamed inside your head, the reality would turn out to be a let down, another bread and marg day, just when you were expecting a feast. I should never have gone searching for the celebrations when the party had packed up and gone home, the partygoers surfeited by so much frivolous, transitory pleasure. The laughing, jiving girls had vanished. I would have to look for them in some other place. Soon the Japs would surrender, then it would be goodbye to the war, goodbye to Winston. Hitler was dead and burning in hell. It was time to think of other things.

* * *

I was nearly fourteen, old enough to become a worker. Soon I would have to look for a job. Ernie had already lost the tip of a finger in an accident at the pit. He waggled the bandaged stump at me in glee when I made a rare visit to his house. "I'm a proper miner now," he chuckled. "All my oppoes have had accidents. You aren't a real miner 'til you've claimed compo for summat missing!"

He had lost interest in me. He would talk of nothing but the pit, his oppoes (mates), the minutia of his day hundreds of feet below ground. I grew bored with his endless tales of life in that nether world, reports on what this oppo had said, what this oppo had done, and most of his tale expressed in words I couldn't understand because it was the language of the pit. Mo had started work as an errand lad in a hosiery dye works. He raced about the factory pushing a wicker hamper on wheels, unloaded vans, and thought it a great life – even more fun than being a Grenadier Guard. At least the job had stopped him fretting about growing tall. I saw little of either of them, but when I did they were cool and disdainful. I was still a mere schoolboy. What did I know of the excitement of working in a man's world?

Mam was determined that I would leave school that Christmas of 1945, even though my fourteenth birthday didn't fall until the first week of the new year. I pleaded to be allowed to stay on until the following Easter. I was enjoying school. I had somehow become a prefect, and one of the headmaster's "blue-eyed boys", but Mam was determined that I would learn what the real world was all about as soon as possible. Another pay packet coming into the house, no matter how small, would provide a slender lifeline as she struggled, up to the neck in debt. She saw little value in education. "They don't teach you owt worth knowing, anyway," she always said. "You'll learn a sight more when you get to work."

I resigned myself to joining Ernie and Mo in their man's world at Christmas. But I was determined to fight against the kind of job she wanted me to take. "You want a piece-work job so you can earn some decent money." She said. "Your Dad'll get you on at the Raleigh. There's lads there earning thirty bob a week."

I knew some of the lads she meant. They were from the rough top-end of Broxtowe, lads out of the bottom classes at school. Like Ernie, they could barely read. They either worked at the Raleigh, or firms like it, or went down the pit. They really had no choice: it was what was expected of them, what their fathers did, what school had trained them for. Nothing else was expected of them. Working somewhere like the Raleigh factory was the future I dreaded most. "I'm not working there!" I protested. "I want to learn a trade." I had no idea what trade I could learn. None of them really interested me. And apprentices were paid starvation wages. It was years before they earned an average wage, and Mam wanted money from me *now*.

"I've been keeping you long enough!" she shouted. "Tradesmen are ten-a-penny. The lads at the Raleigh earn twice as much. You're going there, and that's all there is to it!"

"I'm not working at that dump!" I yelled back every time we argued about a job for me, which was almost every day. "I want to learn a proper trade!"

"You'll do what I say," Mam raged. "It's time you paid summat back for being kept all these years. I want summat off you for a change!"

"I didn't ask you to keep me," I said, uselessly. "It's what you're supposed to do!"

"And lads are supposed to help their mams. That's what kids are for when they're old enough. The Raleigh'll knock that leariness out of you, an'all. That's where you're going, so shut up about it!"

The argument grew more intense as the day of my leaving school approached. Every day was tainted by anger. The more Mam insisted that I go to work at the Raleigh factory, the more defiant I grew until we ended up shouting at each other and I stormed out. I stayed out of the house until hunger drove me back again. Mam would stop talking to me for a few hours, and that was a relief, although she thought it was a punishment. There was no-one I could talk to. My Radford relations would think it odd to make so much fuss about becoming an unskilled factory hand. In the Buttress family, only Aunt Violet understood my reluctance to follow in Dad's footsteps, but I saw little of her. Dad said nothing. He wasn't interested where I worked. As far as he was concerned that was Mam's business, like running the house. He considered his task finished when he handed over a few pound notes out of his wages to pay for groceries.

Mam always ended our rows by claiming that I was in debt to her for being fed and clothed for thirteen years. That hurt so much that I couldn't defend myself with words, and would run upstairs to shed tears of anger and frustration. Her accusation only made me more determined not to work at the Raleigh factory, even if I had to run away from home to avoid it. I didn't want to become one of the Broxtowe lads who worked there, or at the pit. I knew that I would end up like Dad if I did. He hated his job of piecework drudgery at the Raleigh, but worked there because the wages were so much higher than those of a bus conductor. Only his lack of interest in me made it possible for me to stand up to Mam. If he had insisted that I work at the Raleigh factory, I would not be able to resist the two-pronged attack. As it was, all he said was: "It's good money, but it don't suit everybody," and he meant that it wouldn't suit me, which was as near as he got to showing concern.

I was dumb with self-pity when I wasn't arguing with Mam. I brooded on the hateful words about my debt, dramatising it as though I was the innocent victim in some movie about cruel parents and a misused child. I've been eating her dinners every day, I told myself, putting on new shoes and clothes bought with a cheque off the tallyman, and all the time my debt had been piling up without my knowing about it. She's practically accused me of cheating because I won't pay back the debt by working at that lousy factory. There were times when I hated her, too absorbed by pity for myself to understand the pressure that had driven her to say such things, tormented as she was by *never* having enough money to get her through the week without begging and borrowing. I couldn't understand that it was her despair that made me the victim of her angry words against me.

At the heart of her desperation was Dad's selfishness, and his meanness. If Mam borrowed a shilling for the gas meter he would stop it out of her housekeeping allowance the following week. If she was driven to sending me down to the pawnshop tucked behind Whiting's clothes store with a pair of blankets, Dad raged because such transactions were fit only for those with no pride, like the "riff-raff" at the top end of the estate. He had never given Mam a present – or any of his children as far as I remember. He resented Mam treating herself to a new, cheap print frock for her occasional night out to the pub. As his wages increased, her share remained at the same inadequate sum, and no amount of arguing would make him increase it. The paltry amount I would hand over to Mam when I started work would hardly relieve the strain she was under as she tried to feed and clothe herself and the five children in the family – for now my brother, David, had been born. But, absorbed by the self-regard of the young adolescent, I could feel only resentment for having so much responsibility forced upon me. It wasn't my fault I was born I reasoned on long, solitary walks through peaceful Strelley. I shouldn't be in debt for the food she gave me, or the clothes I wore. I never asked for anything apart from money to go to the cinema when I couldn't fiddle it for myself. I didn't even ask for a radio because I knew it was hopeless. I walked to Aunt Edie's house in Bilborough if I wanted to listen to dance music. My boy's wages wouldn't stop us being poorer than we should have been, I complained to myself. She should give up puffing her Woodbines and risking the rent money on hopeless nags running at Newmarket. Sometimes I could see no way our poverty could be changed as long as Dad didn't care. It seemed it was what Mam's stars had decided, the way things were. We would continue to be patronized by Dad's family, always ignored by the toffee-nosed neighbours who thought we belonged at the top end of the estate alongside the "scruffs", always chased by tallymen, the rentman and the lower ranks of bureaucracy. But I dreamed of changing things for myself – I had no idea how, yet, but I had confidence in my stubbornness, an arrogance that somehow I was brighter than the lads who were content to go down the pit, or work at the Raleigh factory. It gave me a confidence that Mam, Aunt Mabel and my sister Brenda called my "leariness", and was the source of much irritation to them. What I was certain of was that if I gave in to Mam I would be pushed into becoming the labourer the Radford family usually bred.

180

The trouble was, I didn't know what I wanted to do. The choices were limited: the jobs the visiting careers officer brought into school gave details of factory jobs, only. The dunces were directed to labouring, those with a few brains being offered the more skilled work such as training for lathe operating or carpentry. My first step into the world of work was clear enough: I would choose my own job in defiance of Mam, then lurch into the future from that hard won position. The advantage of being a fourteen year old from an elementary school was that I would be presumed ignorant, with not a lot in terms of intelligence and ambition expected of me. Therefore, I could only rise in the world. I might even finish up with a job behind a desk, and go home at night with my hands as clean as when I set out in the morning. As for my debt, Mam could sing for it. The cost of repaying it by clocking on at the Raleigh factory for a life of lever pulling was too great. I would end up like Dad, and I was determined to go in the opposition direction. The tranquillity of Strelley village was conducive to such adolescent dreams, and I would swagger home recharged for the next round of the fight with Mam.

In the end, I won the battle with her. I took a card home from the careers officer which gave details of a job with a firm which offered full training as a sewing machine mechanic, a skilled occupation with some kudos to it. In spite of Mam's contempt for such a trade, she gave in at last, though not without a sulky dismissal of it as a "tupenny ha'penny" prospect. She refused to accompany me to the interview, so Dad went with me as it was necessary for a parent to be there. I was offered the job, but the wage was only one pound a week. "Your Mam won't have that," he said as we made our way home. I could see he was a bit surprised by the impression I'd made. "It might be a good job later on. But a pound a week ..." He shook his head, and I knew I would never become a sewing machine mechanic.

He was right: Mam scoffed at a pound a week. "That's no bleddy good to me," she said.

A few days later I polished my shoes, put on my good shirt again and went into the Lace Market, an area of Victorian factories and warehouses close to Nottingham city centre. A pal who had left school in the Summer told me about the printing firm where he worked, and

I went in search of it because they were looking for a trainee. I found it down a tiny, cramped side-street, tucked away behind a six-storey warehouse. The brick was blackened by ninety years of soot. It looked a dump on the outside, and the inside was like a neglected museum, but the wage was five shillings more than the sewing machine job.

When school broke up for the Christmas holiday, my school career was over. On the morning following Boxing Day I pushed open the dirty brown door of Priestly & Swann, Printers, Bookbinders & Boxmakers. It was seven days before my fourteenth birthday – an illegal entry into the world of work! A sour faced office wallah showed me where to hang my jacket, then led me up stone steps between flaking lime-washed walls into a confusing cacophony of clacking printing machines, the air acrid with the smell of chemicals. Two middle-aged women sat at an old wooden bench sticking strips of white paper over creased cardboard, creating shallow boxes with a speed that could only have come after a lifetime of practice. An endless canvas belt smeared with toffee-coloured glue passed slowly before them. They cast the briefest of looks in my direction, then carried on with their nimble-fingered box making, the gossip uninterrupted.

"Here's the new lad," the office wallah informed them. "Do as they tell you," he said to me, and he made it sound like a warning. He walked off, leaving me feeling totally lost and ill at ease.

"Get the lid off that tub," one of the women said bossily. "We're running short of glue."

I struggled to prise the obdurate lid from off what looked like the apple barrel I had once kept a rabbit in. The women tut-tutted impatiently as I fumbled, stupidly. Finally, I managed to lift the lid and peered inside the barrel. The glue had the colour and consistency of caramel, but it smelled foul because it was made from animal bones.

"Give it a good stir," one of the women said, nodding towards a broomstick leaning against their bench. "And mek haste 'cos we're waiting."

I began to stir the thick glue, the stiffness of it hurting my upper arms. I had just become a worker.

* * *

At the end of the week Mam treated me to the pictures because it was my birthday. My four shillings "spending" money out of my first week's wages lay untouched in my pocket. I went to the Forum with Billy to celebrate this marvellous financial independence. Waiting in the queue as cold rain slanted into us, I felt the cherished coins, counting them by touch in my pocket. I had been at work for a week, and the world was different. I stirred obnoxious glue, swept splintering wooden floors, fed paper into a lining machine that must have been a hundred years old, ran errands for the office wallah, fetched fish and chips for the two box making women, and jumped like a March hare when the alcoholic who owned the place shouted an order. The printers and bookbinders were old men who had spent their working lives at the firm. They were good-humoured, helpful and patient. Quietly spoken craftsmen, they were the sort Mam had said were "ten a penny". They seemed to remember what being at work for the first time was like, and helped me through the week.

The office wallah belonged to the past, too. He wore linen guards on his sleeves and sat at a high stool in front of a sloping desk. His domain was a counting house of Victorian office furniture and shelves that hadn't been dusted for years. Like the rest of the place, his corner smelled of mice and decay. He chivvied and chased me, nagged and complained. I hated him, but he seemed to expect that: it was part of the firm's tradition for the staff to be at war with the workers. I wanted to go forward now that I was at work, but I had stepped back into the past.

Apart from the unpleasant box makers and the office wallah, work wasn't so bad, although the ten hour days seemed interminable and I was the lowest form of life – which was a shock after rising to become a "blue-eyed" boy at school. My lowest point was when I had to push a rattling, flatbed handcart over the cobblestones of the Lace Market streets between factories and warehouses which towered with claustrophobic oppression, keeping the district in semi-darkness. I transported hand-bound bookkeeping ledgers the size and weight of encyclopaedias to offices in the city, acutely self-conscious as people stared at this old-fashioned mode of delivering goods. Pushing the handcart made me feel like a hawker on the flog, and I remembered

Ernie and his firewood round. "Please don't let any good-looking girls see me!" I prayed.

I wanted to learn how to bind the ledgers, not push them through the crowded streets like an apprentice peddlar. Bookbinding looked such a beautiful art, I wondered if my clumsy fingers were up to it. I wanted to make up a page with the tiny pieces of metal type Mr Holland, the compositor, expertly built up into something that could be read. That was magic. Impatient, I wanted to take the next step up the ladder after the first week. I might not know where I was going, but I was clear about what I wanted to leave behind.

* * *

The queue outside the Forum shuffled forward in the January drizzle as the commissionaire swung back the glass doors for the five o'clock show. It was time to keep my date with the lovely Claudette Colbert, whom I secretly lusted over in the narcotic darkness of my favourite place. A lad whom I knew was still at school clowned behind me, opening his mouth to catch rain-water trickling from an overflowing gutter. His pal was trying to ignore this daftness. He had left school the same time as me, and he looked miserable, finally losing his temper with his giggling friend. "You'll stop acting stupid when you leave school," he whinged. "You'll have to grow up and stop being daft."

He was beaten already. He sounded like Dad. "It's time you had more sense," he was still telling me. But I knew he was wrong. Look where having sense had got him. I was going to hang on to being daft a little while longer, and meanwhile the beautiful Claudette was waiting for me.